THE
OVERCOMING
MULTIPLE SCLEROSIS
COOKBOOK

THE
OVERCOMING
MULTIPLE SCLEROSIS
COOKBOOK

DELICIOUS RECIPES *for* LIVING WELL *on a* LOW SATURATED FAT DIET

INGRID ADELSBERGER
CONSULTING EDITOR: JACK McNULTY

Foreword by **PROFESSOR GEORGE JELINEK**

ALLEN&UNWIN
SYDNEY · MELBOURNE · AUCKLAND · LONDON

Note: As the Australian Food Standards Code prohibits using a 'gluten-free' claim on oat-containing products, we have not specified 'gluten-free rolled (porridge) oats' in the recipes in this book. However, in Europe and the United States, oats can be marketed as 'gluten-free'.

Allen & Unwin
83 Alexander Street
Crows Nest NSW 2065
Australia
Phone: (61 2) 8425 0100
Email: info@allenandunwin.com
Web: www.allenandunwin.com

Cataloguing-in-Publication details are available
from the National Library of Australia
www.trove.nla.gov.au

ISBN 978 1 76011 374 2

Internal design by Kate Frances Design
Index by Puddingburn Publishing Services
Set in 9.5/15 pt Caecilia LT Std by Post Pre-press Group, Australia
Printed and bound in Australia by SOS Print + Media Group

10 9 8 7 6 5 4 3 2 1

The paper in this book is FSC® certified. FSC® promotes environmentally responsible, socially beneficial and economically viable management of the world's forests.

OVEN GUIDE: You may find cooking times vary depending on the oven you are using. For fan-forced ovens, as a general rule, set the oven temperature to 20°C (70°F) lower than indicated in the recipe.

CONTENTS

Foreword by George Jelinek ix

Introduction 1

Summary of the nutritional approach
recommended on the OMS Recovery Program 4

My story 5

How to use this cookbook 8

Tips and tricks of the OMS cooking style 10

OMS menu plan 32

Advice from a nutritionist 33

Breakfast 35

Snacks and energy bars 49

Starters and salads 61

Soups 93

Tofu and tempeh dishes 113

Fish and shellfish 123

Vegetables 147

Burgers 165

Grains, pasta and noodles 173

One-pot meals 189

Sides 201

Sauces, dressings and toppings 213

Breads, quickbreads and piecrusts 233

Sweets 241

Afterword 270

Acknowledgements 272

Index 274

FOREWORD

Well, it is finally here! For nearly two decades I have been promoting a plant-based wholefood diet plus seafood as the optimal dietary approach to overcoming multiple sclerosis (MS). Over that time, I have received countless requests to produce a cookbook so people with MS can easily access recipes for wholesome, delicious food that is in keeping with these guidelines. Although I cook such food regularly, I have resisted because my expertise is in science, not cooking. The definitive OMS cookbook had to wait for the right person, someone with passion, enthusiasm and a love of food, and importantly, someone with the drive to initiate and stick with the project through the inevitable ups and downs of such an important endeavour. Enter Ingrid Adelsberger! Not only did Ingrid propose and initiate the cookbook, she personally road-tested every recipe in the book . . . no small achievement.

Ingrid was ably supported by Jack McNulty and Sandra Perry. Sandra attended the first ever OMS retreat run outside Australia, in New Zealand in 2007, and Ingrid and Jack attended the first retreat run outside Australasia. In July 2013, OMS broke new ground when Dr Sandra Neate, Dr Craig Hassed and I facilitated the first UK retreat at Launde Abbey in Leicestershire, inspiring not only a lifelong bond between those who attended but also the creation of this wonderful cookbook. With the help of our willing publishers at Allen & Unwin, we decided that a crowd-sourced recipe book was the ideal way to create this resource for people with MS, reflecting the real-life cooking and eating experiences of our expanding group of people overcoming MS worldwide.

With Jack's experience as a professional chef providing culinary oversight, and Sandra's nutritional knowledge ensuring appropriate dietary oversight, Ingrid drove the project from day one, proceeding to garner the best of the submitted offerings from the international OMS group. And aren't they beauties! From breakfast to snack and energy bar ideas, soups, salads, sides and seriously healthy seafood dishes, through to the category people with MS ask about most often—desserts! Yes, a range of delicious OMS-friendly sweets rounds out what I am sure will become a very practical and much-used addition to the OMS kitchen.

But there is much more than that. Ingrid provides good advice, based on personal experience, about one's approach to food and what we eat, how to substitute healthy for unhealthy ingredients, how to set up a kitchen and pantry, and a variety of cooking methods that might need a bit of tweaking to ensure food is optimally healthy.

In our quest to bring the tools enabling recovery to as many people with MS as we can, we at OMS strongly endorse this important new resource for the OMS family. Supported by wonderful information on nutrition and step-by-step instructional videos on how to prepare some of these dishes on the OMS website, the barriers to adopting the OMS dietary approach that some may encounter should now be much easier to overcome.

Ingrid, Jack and Sandra, you have done a wonderful job in getting this collection of mouth-watering and wholesome recipes together. Now to start trying some of them out . . .

Be well.

Professor George Jelinek
Founder of Overcoming Multiple Sclerosis

INTRODUCTION

The *Overcoming Multiple Sclerosis Cookbook* has been written for people living with multiple sclerosis, especially for those following Professor George Jelinek's Overcoming Multiple Sclerosis Recovery Program.

About the Overcoming Multiple Sclerosis diet

The Overcoming Multiple Sclerosis (OMS) diet is a plant-based wholefood diet with seafood and very low saturated fat.

Several long-term studies show a close connection between saturated fats and the development and progression of multiple sclerosis (MS). For people with MS who avoid saturated fats (such as meat or dairy fat) but consume unsaturated fats (such as those from fish and flaxseed) the progression of the disease is typically reduced; in many cases they experience minimal effects from the disease.

The OMS diet is a very healthy diet for the whole family, unless a family member has other special dietary needs. It is likely to prevent many chronic Western diseases. Professor Jelinek advises that the recipes in this book and the OMS diet may also be beneficial for people with a variety of chronic Western diseases, including inflammatory, degenerative and auto-immune diseases, such as heart disease, high blood pressure, type 2 diabetes, lupus and rheumatoid arthritis.

Why do we need a special cookbook for people with MS?

No other type of cookbook completely caters to the needs of people following the OMS diet. With the *Overcoming Multiple Sclerosis Cookbook* you can be confident that every recipe fully complies with the OMS diet.

Once you become familiar with cooking in the OMS style, you'll be able to adapt other recipes and create your own new ones.

Where do the recipes and tips come from?

The recipes and tips in this cookbook have been 'crowdsourced', contributed by people all around the world who are following the OMS Recovery Program.

You'll see the name of each contributor at the top of each recipe and also where they live.

Everyone who has shared a recipe or a tip is helping to make it easier for others to enjoy tasty meals on the OMS diet and to follow the diet guidelines at home, at work and when eating out.

Measurements in the recipes appear in both metric and imperial.

The menu plan

Also included, on page 32, is a menu plan for a week, using recipes that appear in the book. The menu plan shows how you can create a nutritionally balanced diet while following the OMS Recovery Program.

More information about Overcoming Multiple Sclerosis

For a complete explanation of Professor George Jelinek's OMS diet and his research-based approach to lifestyle management, see his book, *Overcoming Multiple Sclerosis: The evidence-based 7 step recovery program*, 2nd edition, Allen & Unwin, 2016. You can also find further information on the OMS website and join the international OMS community here: https://overcomingms.org/

Who are we?

AIngrid Adelsberger is a home cook and the editor of the *Overcoming Multiple Sclerosis Cookbook*. She was diagnosed with MS in 2011 and discovered OMS the same year. After successfully following the diet for about a year, Ingrid was still struggling emotionally with being unable to eat the food she loved and fell off the wagon. She wondered if cooking better tasting food would make it easier to stick to the diet, and so the idea of a cookbook for the OMS community was born.

Since her diagnosis, Ingrid has been interested in the benefits of nutrition, meditation and fitness. She is now a yoga instructor and a health coach, helping other people to create a sustainable happy and healthy lifestyle.

Born in Vienna, Austria, Ingrid lived in New York City for over a decade before moving to Los Angeles with her husband in 2016. Ingrid has been successfully managing her MS on the OMS program since 2011.

Jack McNulty is a professional chef and has taken the role of consulting editor for the cookbook. Since 2004 he and his wife Silvia have run a popular food and wine business in Zurich, Switzerland, offering catering and cooking courses. He has been following the OMS program since 2009 and some of his recipes appear in the *Overcoming Multiple Sclerosis Cookbook* and on the OMS website.

Sandra Perry is a clinical nutritionist from New Zealand, currently living with her husband in Shenzhen, China. She has been following the OMS program since 2007 when she attended the first OMS retreat held in New Zealand. Sandra has run her own private practice and has worked closely with the Auckland MS Society, running nutrition seminars as well as helping members to integrate the OMS diet into their lives.

SUMMARY OF THE NUTRITIONAL APPROACH RECOMMENDED ON THE OMS RECOVERY PROGRAM

Eat plant-based wholefoods plus seafood, the optimal nutrition to prevent MS progression.

Embrace this as a permanent life change rather than a diet, which implies it is temporary.

Start by emptying out the pantry of all the old foods and start with a clean slate.

Substitute healthy foods for the unhealthy ones that contain dairy products and saturated fats.

Regularly add cold-pressed flaxseed oil to food after cooking and before eating.

There is no need to count grams of saturated fat in foods.

Avoid frying with oil; instead, dry-fry or stir-fry with water or steam.

George Jelinek, *Overcoming Multiple Sclerosis*,
2nd edition, Allen & Unwin, 2016

MY STORY

I heard about MS for the first time when I was about ten years old. I went to a Catholic school and every year each class would raise money for a good cause. A teacher had mentioned a woman who was suffering from MS and described the disease as a horrible one where you watch yourself deteriorate. That year we raised money for her. Over the next two decades, I also witnessed someone close to me living with MS. People have a general perception about the disease which still exists today: it's one where you end up in a wheelchair. Needless to say, I was shocked when I was diagnosed with MS in March 2011, as I had always lived life with a 'that's not happening to me' attitude. I was determined that I would not end up watching myself deteriorate. I was 30 years old, working as an event planner in New York City, and having to deal with such a death sentence made me feel very alone; even though I had a great support system of friends, I missed my family at that time.

For months before I was diagnosed I had tingling in my fingers and arms that eventually moved to the upper right side of my body, where sensations of cold and heat did not feel the same as on my left side. That scared me enough to finally see a neurologist. I remember sitting at my desk at work when the neurologist called to tell me they had found lesions in my spinal cord and thought it was MS. It was confirmed two weeks later when the second MRI showed lesions in my brain. I remember scrambling to find a piece of paper and a pen, asking, 'How do you spell lesions?'

I then went to a neurologist specialising in MS who, not surprisingly, recommended injections of MS medicines, including either Copaxone or Betaserone. When researching different drugs, I learned that they don't cure anything; there's just a chance they will reduce the number of possible relapses. This information made me step back to see what other options I had.

After a few months of anger, depression and a bit of self-pity, I started to search the internet for possible answers and came across Dr Swank's diet. In the Swank forum, Professor Jelinek's name came up so often that I looked him up, and that led me to the OMS diet. His explanations of the science made a lot of sense to me. I decided to follow the OMS diet that same day.

As a child I had bread with Nutella or some sort of pastry almost every day for breakfast. My lunch at school most days was meat- and carb-heavy and, even though my mother paid attention to cooking balanced home-cooked meals, as is typical in our culture, they were meat- and carb-heavy too, and fish and vegetables were not on my list of favourites. Therefore, giving up more food items after already following the Swank diet for a month was not easy for me; in fact I resisted it. When I started on the Swank and then the OMS diet, I was already on an elimination diet, as I had read much about the possible onset and causes of MS and thought a clean eating plan could be helpful. So I cut out everything that was on the 'avoid' list within a week or two.

The hardest things for me to avoid were chocolate and pastries, as these were a big part of my daily diet. I also thought it would be hard to never eat meat again, but my true struggle came with sweets. For about one year, I followed the diet very rigorously. Living in New York City and eating out or ordering in most nights made it a challenge to find suitable food, so I decided to cook at home. The results were mostly bland.

After about a year of being on the diet, I developed pneumonia which, luckily, did not lead to a relapse; however, my spirits were really down. In that time, my emotions about my MS and what I could not eat made me really struggle with everything and I fell into a depression. So, one sad night I had some chocolate. And then the next day some more. Unfortunately, it didn't end there. I struggled with the diet for about six months. That resulted in various cheats with pastries, chocolate and other non-OMS-friendly foods. The peak of this depression was a week-long business trip where I ate everything (except meat) that I could get my hands on. I felt ashamed and defeated.

It took another four to five months, more mishaps with eating, personal development workshops and ultimately an OMS retreat to get me out of that self-destructive phase. In that time, I wondered whether cooking tastier meals and snacks for myself would give me a better chance of sticking to the OMS diet. Being in a new relationship helped as well, as I needed to make enjoyable food that my partner and I could share together. And the idea for a cookbook for the OMS community was born.

I am neither a cook nor a nutritionist. I am just a normal person with MS making a dietary life change. On my journey I have become aware of the link between food and emotions: food is not just nutrition we put into our body when we eat, it's part of our culture, social life, memories. I can see how my emotions have influenced my food choices ever since I was a child—for example, eating sweets when I was sad. For a healthy and happy life, I realised that I can work on these emotions to reduce or even eliminate the resulting cravings for sweets or fancy meals, and that I can also change the 'reward system' and replace the reward with an OMS-friendly treat. This is what we are focusing on in this cookbook. To do this, I needed to be more creative in the kitchen and make meals and snacks that satisfied me and kept me below the 10 g (¼ oz) of saturated fat. When I started on the diet I could not even begin to imagine that I would never be able to have a croissant with Nutella again. Sometimes I still feel sad that I can't, but now I make myself something deliciously similar that is OMS-friendly. These discoveries about my emotions and reworking my reward system have been very useful tools.

Food is important—it is our medicine and our nutrition; it can help people with MS to stay well. I believe that enjoying and sharing food with friends and family and always being able to come up with a nice-tasting meal when needed are as important as the nutrition itself for our wellbeing, as it empowers us to lead active, fulfilling lives. My wish and goal is to create many meals that are both nutritious and enjoyable. This book is a collection of recipes from the OMS community to the OMS community that taste good, keep you well and make you happy. I have included a broad selection with many different ingredients from different cultures as well as both simple and challenging recipes. There is something for everyone.

HOW TO USE THIS COOKBOOK

In 2016, Professor George Jelinek released the second edition of his book *Overcoming Multiple Sclerosis: The evidence-based 7 step recovery program* in which he explains the causes of multiple sclerosis and the research evidence for the Overcoming Multiple Sclerosis Recovery Program for staying well while living with MS. His book emphasises the importance of a diet low in saturated fats. It provides suggestions for handling oils—the amounts, how to cook with them, which food groups to eat or to avoid and much more. It is recommended to read his book before you use this cookbook, as the science and the other information in the program will give an essential overview of the OMS lifestyle and why certain cooking methods and food choices are as important as they are.

This cookbook, in combination with the science, will help you. It focuses on how to incorporate the changes you will need to make in your daily life by giving suggestions about cooking and diet. It takes some time to learn the ins and outs of the OMS lifestyle and then more time to use them day-by-day. I found it quite challenging to relearn cooking methods and change my eating habits, and I truly hope that the information I share here will make it easier for you.

This book also gives ideas and suggestions on topics and situations I struggled the most with:

- how to find recipes
- how to substitute ingredients for OMS-friendly options
- how to stock up the pantry with healthy food
- what kitchen equipment I found useful on my OMS cooking path
- cuisines I find most OMS-friendly when eating out
- meals and snacks to eat outside of home.

Furthermore, I discovered that some humour and creativity are most useful. I had situations where I pitied myself for not being able to eat something that everyone else could and cheated. Today, in these moments, I try to be creative. There is almost always food in that fridge, on that table, in that restaurant that fits our dietary restrictions. And if there really is nothing, I remind myself why I'm eating the way I am and that the things I am not eating are foods that could potentially lead me to the wheelchair. And I don't want to go there!

When I wrote these introductory pages I researched much again on the OMS forum and in the OMS book, and had advisory calls with Jack McNulty, a professional chef. Jack and I met in the UK in 2013 when we attended the first European-based OMS retreat with George Jelinek, Dr Sandra Neate and Dr Craig Hassed. Jack has been delighting the OMS community with his extensive knowledge and delicious recipes. During the process of working on this book, I was reminded of many details of the diet part of this program. Some of them were clear to me, others were good to hear again and yet others I remembered only partially or had completely forgotten. Realising that opened my eyes (again). Keeping up with the facts and being clear about them is essential for a positive outcome and stopping the progression of MS.

Dr Swank writes in his book that it's advisable to measure serving sizes from time to time. He also mentions that being 'too' comfortable on the diet is a slippery slope, so being mindful and aware of what we eat is also important as we continue on this life change. Therefore, although those of us on the OMS diet do not count saturated fat on a daily basis, I do find it helpful to check it from time to time.

As the recipes are from various OMSers in many countries, certain ingredients may vary. One example is tofu. First, in each country there is a softer and a firmer version but the texture may differ. Another one is nutritional yeast: the American version has a deeper yellow colour and richer 'cheese-like' flavour than the yeast you buy in Europe. Non-dairy yoghurts and milks will also differ in flavour, sugar content and possible added fillers. Flour is milled differently in each country and may change the outcome of a recipe slightly. These variations should not be seen as a challenge; they simply make our life change to OMS-friendly foods more interesting and exciting.

TIPS AND TRICKS OF THE OMS COOKING STYLE

How to find recipes that fit the OMS diet

When I was growing up in Austria I loved banana cake—it consisted of sponge cake, vanilla cream, bananas and a chocolate shell on top. I made that cake once by replacing milk with plant-based milk, eggs with egg whites and a few teaspoons of oil instead of butter, and in place of the chocolate shell I dusted the top with cacao powder. Granted the cake didn't look exactly the same and the consistency of the cream was different but everybody who tasted it (including non-vegan, non-OMS-friendly friends) seemed to like it.

After being on the diet for a year or two and eating boring meals, I longed to cook and taste good food again. At first I didn't know where to start, as it seemed that every recipe I found in cookbooks and on the internet included ingredients that are on the OMS 'avoid' list or use unsuitable cooking methods. As I started to experiment in the kitchen, I realised there were a few ways to both come up with and find recipes. Normally, two situations sparked my curiosity: a dish I remembered from pre-OMS times, or a vegan recipe I liked but that used an unsuitable amount or type of oil, or too many nuts.

If it is a regular recipe (meaning non-vegan), the ingredients to be replaced are meat, dairy or oil, or the cooking method should be changed. When making cakes or pastries, chocolate is often involved too. In some recipes, particularly when it comes to baking, certain ingredients are important for consistency as well as flavour. For example, if a cake is made with butter and you replace it with oil, it mostly works. But icing needs the saturated fat of butter for stability, so replacing it with oil doesn't work. If you are an inexperienced cook, as I was, it can take some time to realise what can and can't be done. The more I tried and failed, the easier the search for recipes became, and I figured out much faster what could be reworked to become an OMS-friendly meal. This resulted in fewer disasters in the kitchen and more interesting meals.

When the recipe is a vegan one, you often need to replace the coconut oil or the quantity of nuts. Many vegan recipes (especially desserts) use coconut oil or margarine instead of butter for stability. If coconut oil is used for its stability, then following the OMS guidelines and replacing it is very hard, if not impossible, as the coconut oil makes the dish stable when it cools down and helps the ingredients bind. Another option is to add a vegan stabiliser such as agar-agar, xanthan gum or guar gum. If coconut is used for flavour, the combination of plant-based milk and coconut extract is a good replacement.

In many recipes the dishes are made in a way that is not suitable for us. For example, we should avoid frying or sautéing in oil and instead fry in water or dry-fry. Baking is safer than frying, but we should still be aware of the amount of oil (if any) in the recipe. Frying heats the oil to a very high temperature very quickly. Baking, on the other hand, is a more controlled method of heat transfer. Imagine putting your hand in a pot of boiling water or frying oil: it would hurt immediately and you would have to pull it out at once. But when you stick your hand into an oven heated to a temperature of, let's say, 200°C (400°F/gas 6), you can leave your hand there for a few moments without burning it.

In many cases, using a small amount of oil in baking is okay, especially if liquid is an ingredient, but we still need to be careful about how much we use. With time and experience you'll learn that oils are not even necessary in many dishes.

So when looking at a recipe, make sure that oil is omitted whenever possible. When you do use oil, check it has been stored correctly and is in best condition, then adjust the cooking method so there is minimal cell oxidation of the oil. For example, when you make a pasta sauce, dry-fry the onions and garlic before adding the tomatoes, herbs and spices, etc. When it is ready to be served, you can add a bit of high quality extra virgin olive oil or flaxseed oil if you wish.

Substitutions

Here are some ideas for substitutions in cooking and baking that should ease your transition into the OMS-friendly eating lifestyle.

Chocolate

Chocolate can be very easily replaced by cacao powder. When you start on the diet, you may feel that cacao powder isn't as sweet and strong in flavour as chocolate; however, over time your taste will change and you will not feel deprived anymore. Personally, I do not use more than ¼ cup of cacao powder, no matter what the recipe calls for, and only very rarely on special occasions will

I go up to ½ cup. I have also noticed that adding some ingredients with texture, such as crushed nuts, poppy seeds or ground rolled (porridge) oats, makes a nice addition and will not be too high in saturated fat in a regular slice of cake.

Coconut

Coconut oil and coconut milk contain high amounts of saturated fat and therefore are not part of the OMS diet. Coconut oil is frequently found in recipes for vegan desserts and some Asian dishes and needs to be replaced. As far as the flavour goes, coconut extract can be added and then combined with either soy yoghurt or a plant-based milk—for example, in stews and soups. In baking, it depends on the recipe because coconut is often used for stability. If you want to use coconut for flavour, as I've already mentioned, the combination of coconut extract and plant-based milk works really well.

Dairy products

Butter

As far as consistency goes, butter is hard to replace completely; however, there are some good substitutions depending on what it is needed for.

Butter on bread

If you enjoy a piece of bread with butter, flaxseed oil or extra virgin olive oil may be used. Personally, I like flaxseed oil in combination with honey or jam, but if that is not palatable, straight jam or honey will do the trick too. It may be something you will need to get used to but after a while you will not miss butter. You could also use raw nut or seed butters such as almond, cashew, hazelnut, walnut and tahini (sesame).

If you are looking for savoury spreads, hummus, baba ghanoush, lentil pâté or mashed avocado are good on toast.

Butter in baking

Butter is used in many cake recipes because it is a stable fat (for example, for buttercream icing) and finding a good substitute is not easy. In baking, extra virgin olive oil or apple sauce may be suitable. Depending on the recipe, you could experiment with vegan binders such as xanthan gum, arrowroot or guar gum.

Cheese

When I started on the OMS diet it seemed inconceivable that I would never eat cheese again but now, after all these years, I wouldn't eat cheese even if I could. There are brands of vegan cheese available in health food stores but, even if the saturated fat content is low, it is advisable to stay away from them as they are highly processed and many (if not all) contain some sort of refined vegetable oil or tropical fat (palm or coconut). Furthermore, many vegan cheeses also contain potentially harmful fillers. As far as the consistency of biting into a piece of cheese goes, I am not aware of any substitution to be honest; however, there are nut cheese recipes that are really very good. These kinds of cheese are most comparable to French cheese spreads.

When it comes to cooking dishes like sauces, gratins or pasta, I use almond meal for consistency and nutritional yeast for flavour. Nutritional yeast is a great substitute for parmesan.

Ice cream

Ice cream can be easily replaced with dairy-free sorbet. There are some vegan alternatives that may or may not be suitable, depending on the saturated fat content and the type of oil used. Vegan ice cream alternatives can also be made at home with plant-based milk and frozen fruits such as berries or bananas (see the Banana Soft Serve recipe on page 244). They will be much healthier than the ice creams you will find in stores and you can also lower the sugar content.

Milk

You will find milk is one of the easiest ingredients to replace in your diet. Most supermarkets sell soy milk but if that's not for you, you can buy plant-based milk made out of almonds, rice, oat or hemp, to mention just a few, from health food stores. You will eventually work out which types you prefer. For example, I've noticed soy milk curdles in hot coffee yet foams best for my cappuccino. Some plant-based milks have more protein, others more sweetener. I love soy milk in my cappuccino but mostly use almond milk for baking, and rice milk for stews and soups.

Yoghurt

Yoghurt is quite an easy ingredient to substitute these days—there are almond and soy versions available, even hemp, although that is rare. Both almond and soy yoghurt taste very different to dairy yogurts; however, I found that it just took time to get used to them. I use non-dairy yoghurts for baking cakes, or in my muesli and other cereals for breakfast. When making puréed vegetable soups, add plain unsweetened soy yoghurt for great consistency. In yoghurt dips and sauce recipes, dairy yoghurt can be replaced by soy yoghurt and will still be delicious.

Eggs

An omelette can be easily made with egg whites and vegetables and smoked salmon. Another option is a tofu scramble instead of scrambled eggs.

As far as eggs in baking go, you may choose the vegan option and use a flax egg (see page 31) or chia egg (see page 31). Alternatively, you may use two egg whites instead of one egg. These substitutions suit most recipes but, again, if the saturated fat content is needed for stability, they may not work. However, egg white is a very good binder and many delicious desserts can be made with whisked egg whites.

Gelatine

Gelatine can be very easily replaced with agar-agar. Made from sea algae, it has a very similar consistency to gelatine and is completely plant-based. You may find it as an ingredient in vegan sweets. You can buy agar-agar in health food stores and use it in soups, stews, fruit preservatives, desserts and ice creams. One teaspoon of agar flakes or agar powder is equivalent to eight sheets of gelatine. Agar-agar is also firmer than gelatine.

Icing

It is challenging to find a replacement for butter in icing. A stable fat is needed and most, such as margarine, have too much saturated fat. One thing that I've found suitable for icing is avocado. Avocado or nut butter mixed with cacao powder, plant-based milk and sugar or agave nectar are options for special occasion cakes. Another option is to make a flavoured sugar icing such as icing (confectioners') sugar mixed with lemon juice. It is advisable to use these options only rarely as the avocado and nut butter substitutes tend to be high in saturated fat and, although the sugar version is fat-free, it contains a lot of sugar for someone on an ultra-healthy diet.

Meat

Today there are many vegan options for replacing not just plain chicken or beef, but also salami and bologna. Many products are on the low end of saturated fat. However, Professor Jelinek suggests staying away from these as they are highly processed and are often made with soy protein isolate, which is the waste product of soy. Healthier options are tofu, tempeh or seitan. Some are healthier than others, depending on the process (stay away from seitan if you avoid gluten, and from tofu and tempeh if you don't eat soy). If you choose to consume soy products, always purchase organic non-GMO versions if you can. Tofu can be seasoned in the same way as recipes that call for meat.

Oil

Oil in baking

I try to minimise the amount of oil and saturated fat in my diet as much as I can. I bake many recipes with almost no oil but when oil cannot be completely avoided, I search for a version of the recipe that calls for a lower amount, as I know the final dish will work. I almost always downsize the amount of oil and rarely use more than ¼ cup of extra virgin olive oil for a cake. In my early days of baking, I didn't add any olive oil to my cake batters, but after experimenting with moistness and freshness, I realised that some, even 1–2 teaspoons, does help.

To help me cut down on the amount of oil needed in a cake, I use apple sauce or mashed banana. The advantage of apple sauce in comparison to mashed banana is that apple sauce adds sweetness, whereas mashed banana adds a banana taste. Besides those two, plant-based yoghurt can be used for consistency and moistness. In recipes that call for yoghurt, cream or mascarpone, use plant-based yoghurt. Please be aware that OMS-friendly cakes dry out quickly, so it's best to eat them within a day or two. Alternatively, freeze them if you want to keep them for longer.

Oil in cooking

When frying, Professor Jelinek suggests replacing oil with water. Alternatively, you can dry-fry and not use any liquid at all. It is always best to avoid heating oils to reduce the likelihood of oxidation. To enhance flavour, add oil after the cooking process. If you find flaxseed oil palatable, drizzling it over your dishes is the best way to achieve Professor Jelinek's suggested daily intake. If you don't like the taste, try taking supplements or flaxseed oil straight up (or mixed with juice), or add extra virgin olive or sesame oil (to Asian dishes) before serving to enhance flavour.

When purchasing any oil, check the due date to guarantee that you consume the freshest product possible. Oil high in omega-3, such as flaxseed oil and hemp oil, as well as oil high in omega-6 or -9 (sesame, extra virgin olive oil and unrefined rapeseed oil) should always be stored in the fridge.

Spreads and fillings

There are lots of options for creating OMS-friendly sandwich spreads although they may not seem obvious at first. Some vegan spreads have high levels of saturated fat or oil that are not part of our diet, so look for suitable options in health food stores. I have found store-bought spreads, such as hummus, baba ghanoush and bean, lentil or beetroot (beet) dips, made with extra virgin olive oil, that fall within with the OMS guidelines. However, those you make yourself will be healthier.

Another option is tuna or other fish salad. Mayonnaise can be replaced with the recipe in this book (see page 220) or soy yoghurt. Spreading avocado on toast is a lovely breakfast or snack, and extra virgin olive or flaxseed oil can be used on toast too. Storing flaxseed oil in the freezer before it's opened turns it a bit gel-like, which makes it easier to spread. If you miss spreads, you will find a few options in the recipe section—for example, Semi-dried Tomato and Basil Dip (page 62), Baba Ghanoush (page 64), Bean Dip (page 66) and Soy Quark (page 68).

Peanuts

Peanuts are a part of many Southeast Asian savoury dishes, such as pad Thai or papaya salad, and desserts. In the US peanut butter is a staple for kids and grownups in the famous PBJ—peanut butter and jelly sandwich—and is used globally in snacks. High in omega-6, peanuts are pro-inflammatory, susceptible to toxins and one of the most common food allergens. It is advisable to stay away from them and to replace peanut butter with almond butter (the best alternative) or another nut butter, such as hazelnut, almond or cashew butter. You should also replace peanuts with almonds or, depending on the dish, other types of nut, such as cashews or pistachios, but in smaller amounts.

Note: Please be aware that all nuts are high in omega-6 even though they are OMS-safe.

Getting started

When making a life change, we often wonder what we'll need to make the transition as smooth as possible. The OMS lifestyle mainly asks for a positive attitude and some endurance so you can overcome the first hurdles. A well-stocked pantry and possibly some new equipment in the kitchen could make the early stages easier and even more enjoyable.

Kitchen equipment

When I started on the OMS diet, I barely had any equipment in my kitchen, not even great pots, a mixer or a baking tin. And even though I had some very minimal cooking experience, none of it came in handy for OMS cooking.

Over the years, bit by bit, I have acquired a better selection of kitchenware. If you have been cooking pre-OMS, then you will probably already have everything you need. Having the right tools is not a must; however, using them reduces a lot of frustration and makes the healthy cooking and eating experience a much more pleasurable one.

Food processor/blender

At the top of my list is a high-speed blender. It helps me to make desserts, and crushes nuts, oats, dried fruits and other ingredients so much faster than I can chop them. I also use it to make smoothies, soups, sauces, flours, puddings, nut butters and much more. I do not own a food processor; when chopping vegetables I only pulse them quickly so they don't liquefy. If you spend a lot of time in the kitchen, owning one or the other will help you tremendously. I use my blender to make lots of delicious dishes and snacks that follow the OMS guidelines.

Coffee grinder

A coffee grinder is a wonderful and cheap addition to your collection of kitchen equipment as it grinds and chops flaxseeds and small quantities of nuts and herbs and spices. When I don't want or need to use my high-speed blender (or I am only grinding small quantities), I use the coffee grinder.

Steamer insert

Steaming is the cooking method preferred and most often used in this book. A steamer insert that can be used in almost any pan is a very cheap and good investment. I use mine almost every day for steaming vegetables, tofu or fish.

Juicer

These days many wellness or health practitioners believe that juicing is very beneficial for your overall health, so a juicer is another essential item in my kitchen. The models vary in price, size and efficiency, so buy something that will match your juicing habits. A carrot, apple and ginger juice, or a green vegetable juice, is a great way to start the morning.

Knives

A good sharp knife is one item that you will need, as being on a plant-based wholefood diet involves chopping a lot of fruit and vegetables. In the beginning, not having a good-quality knife was very frustrating. My life is much easier now that I've invested in one (or two).

Electric mixer

The first piece of kitchen equipment I bought was a decent mixer. I had not baked much before and when I started, I quickly got tired of beating egg whites by hand. An electric mixer is a must-have for bakers.

Pots and pans

Investing in non-stick pots and pans helps tremendously. As we cook without oil, they make cooking and cleaning up much easier. A non-stick baking dish is also a great addition if you bake regularly.

There has been much discussion about the health hazards associated with cooking with Teflon products in recent years, so it pays to avoid using low-end non-stick pans. A bit of research comes in handy here! I personally may not own a top-notch stainless steel pan but I do own a good mid-range one. Stainless steel pans may be a safe and versatile option for many dishes.

Rice cooker

Having a rice cooker is another fairly cheap investment that will make your life easier. You can cook all grains in it as well as add beans and vegetables for a quick no-oil meal.

Other kitchen gadgets

If you think you will really get into cooking on your OMS path, an ice-cream maker, a bread maker, a slow cooker, a pressure cooker, a dehydrator and a hand mixer can be helpful and fun to have. They are not essential, just gadgets that helped me the most. Lastly, it's very helpful to have a scale at home (preferably a dual one for metric and imperial if you like to search the web for recipe ideas).

Food in my pantry

When I started on the OMS diet I ate steamed vegetables, rice, beans, canned sardines and salad. As I became more familiar with legumes and grains, I began to stock my pantry with ingredients that not so long ago I hadn't known existed.

Here are some of the dry ingredients I almost always have on hand. These items are just suggestions and seem to be the ones that come up the most in a plant-based wholefood diet. As you go along, it's advisable to week by week add an item you often come across in recipes. That way you expand your pantry and don't burst your grocery budget. Once you have built up a good base of grains, spices and legumes, the rest is just icing on the cake.

Grains and pastas
- brown rice
- brown rice pasta
- burghul (bulgur)
- couscous
- millet or amaranth
- polenta (cornmeal)
- quinoa
- risotto or basmati rice
- rolled (porridge) or old-fashioned oats
- whole spelt grain (spelt berries) or whole-wheat grain (wheat berries)
- wholemeal (whole-wheat) pasta

Flours
- almond meal
- spelt flour
- unbleached plain (all-purpose) flour
- wholemeal (whole-wheat pastry) flour

Note: the flours you have at home will vary depending on whether you are gluten-free or not.

Beans/legumes

- black beans
- black lentils
- chickpeas (garbanzo beans)
- green lentils
- red kidney beans
- red lentils
- silken or firm organic, non-GMO tofu, tempeh, seitan (in the fridge)
- split peas

Seeds, nuts (raw) and dried fruit

- almonds (best stored in an airtight container in the fridge)
- cashews (best stored in an airtight container in the fridge)
- chia seeds
- dried cherries
- dried cranberries
- flaxseeds and flaxseed meal (I grind the seeds in the coffee grinder to make my own flaxseed meal and store it in the freezer so the nutrients are retained for a few days)
- hemp seeds
- pepitas (pumpkin seeds)
- raisins
- sunflower seeds
- walnuts

Note: You may not need all of them but having a variety in your pantry is great for snacks, for your porridge (oatmeal) or other cereal in the morning and to spice up salads.

Oils and vinegars

- balsamic vinegar
- cold-pressed extra virgin olive oil
- flaxseed oil (in the fridge)
- raw apple cider vinegar
- rice vinegar
- sesame oil (in the fridge)

Sweeteners

- agave nectar
- dates
- maple syrup
- molasses
- raw sugar

My most used spices and herbs

- cayenne pepper
- chilli flakes
- chilli powder
- dried basil
- dried bay leaves
- dried dill
- dried oregano
- dried rosemary
- dried thyme
- fine and coarse sea salt
- garam masala
- garlic powder
- ground allspice
- ground cardamom
- ground cinnamon and cinnamon sticks
- ground coriander (cilantro) and whole seeds
- ground cumin
- ground ginger
- ground nutmeg
- ground turmeric
- ground and whole cloves
- onion powder
- paprika (sweet, hot and/or smoked)
- Tabasco sauce

Others

- agar-agar

- almond butter
- apple sauce
- baking soda
- cans of sardines in water
- cans of tuna in water
- cornflour (cornstarch) or arrowroot
- matcha powder
- miso paste
- nutritional yeast
- plant-based milk
- seaweed (dried)
- tamari or soy sauce
- tomato passata
- unsweetened cacao powder (make sure it's a low fat one—the fat content can vary hugely)
- vegetable stock or broth (I use a powder that doesn't have any oil)

Buying quality food will very much depend on your financial options and where you live. As we consume mainly fruit, vegetables, grains, legumes and seafood on the OMS diet, we need to buy the best we can afford. Shopping locally and buying organic food in season from multiple sources—farmers' markets, health food stores, greengrocers, fishmongers and sometimes supermarkets—ensures your food is fresher, provides a good mix of nutrients and lowers your exposure to a single pesticide (even organic food can be exposed to pesticides).

Wild-caught fish does not contain antibiotics and is also safer when it comes to pollutants, cancer-causing chemicals and contaminants. Another concern is mercury. Professor Jelinek and other health practitioners suggest eating sardines and other small fish, as they consume mainly plankton and do not accumulate mercury eating other fish.

It's important to educate yourself about salmon (fresh and frozen) and make sure you're buying it from a reliable source. Different breeds of salmon vary hugely in their saturated fat content, which can also be affected by the food they eat. Wild-caught salmon—nearly impossible to buy in Europe these days—is lower in saturated fat than their farmed counterparts.

Cooking methods

When adapting to the OMS cooking style, you need to relearn how to cook and bake. If you are an experienced home cook and have prepared your meals a certain way for a long time, you will need to adjust, but once it becomes a habit, it will not be an issue. I found only a few recipes that really were impossible to adapt to the OMS diet.

Sautéing and stir-frying

There are a few recipes that are almost impossible to fry with just water—for example, an omelette. In these cases, I follow Professor Jelinek's suggestions and use a combination of oil and water. Water boils at 100°C (212°F) and oil at a much higher temperature. By adding water, you reduce the temperature of the oil when it is heated. I often use a spray mister for water and a brush for the oil; that way the oil spreads evenly in the pan and I can minimise the amount I use. However, be aware that the temperature has to be very low, otherwise the oil will splash everywhere and may burn you. This method also minimises the oxidation in the oil.

Here are Jack McNulty's step-by-step instructions for frying with water.

To sweat

Use this method for cooking onions in soups, sauces and stews.

Cook the onions in a heavy-based pan over medium heat until the onions turn translucent. Be sure to add a bit of water if the onions begin to stick too much and take on colour. You are just looking to soften the onions at this stage and remove their raw flavour rather than caramelising them and adding sweetness.

To create colour and flavour

Use this method if you are making a brown sauce, for example. Heat a large heavy-based pan (preferably stainless steel) over medium heat. The pan will have reached the correct temperature when a few drops of water immediately swirl in the pan like mercury balls. At this point, add the chopped onions and season them with salt to help release their water. Allow the onions to stew gently in their juices until they begin to stick to the pan. Release the onions and their juices by adding 1–2 tablespoons of water and gently scraping the pan with a spatula. Continue with the same process until the onions reach a nice golden colour and their juices become brown. This will take 10–15 minutes, so be patient.

Baking and roasting

While working on this cookbook, I realised there is a huge misconception in the OMS community about baking and roasting and its temperature (I had it wrong too!). I believe the misconception comes from the suggested 180°C (350°F/gas 4) that Dr Swank describes as the recommended maximum temperature in his book. Somehow that number made its way to the OMS forum and the conversion of 175°C (350°F/gas 4) came shortly after. I searched the OMS book up and down but couldn't find a reference to the baking temperature . . . because there is none!

Our goal in any cooking process is to reduce the amount of saturated fat in our diet as well as reduce the impact of cell oxidation, which increases if the oil itself is already oxidised while being stored in the grocery store or at home. Oxidation happens naturally when you open, for example, a bottle of extra virgin olive oil (or any other oil, especially the unrefined ones we want to consume). The other way oil gets destroyed is through temperature. That is why the OMS diet recommends not frying with oil: the temperature is so high it destroys the oil.

Baking and roasting is different as, in comparison to frying, the oil gets less damaged (see heat transfer on page 11). However, we still want to minimise the cell oxidation, either through heat or air, as much as possible so we either avoid adding oil or use as little as we can. In addition, due to the evaporation of the moisture as well as the liquid within the food, its surface will not get as hot as the temperature in your oven.

When baking fish, for example, it's important to preserve the natural oil in the fish as much as possible. Bake salmon for 8–10 minutes at 190°C (375°F/gas 5) instead of for 30 minutes at 160°C (315°F/gas 2–3).

It is also good to remember that flour contains wheat germ oil and that any baking with flour involves oil that will be broken down (so, even if you do not add any, there will be some oil). All food contains some oil that will break down a bit, so do not get too worried about it.

Steaming and boiling

Steaming and boiling are the preferred OMS cooking methods (and are healthiest for everyone). They are also the easiest ways to cook without any oil.

I try to steam and boil as much as I can, and the great thing is that it works for almost all food groups: vegetables, grains, legumes, fish and tofu. I always try to steam vegetables, which helps to retain more nutrients than if they are boiled. After preparing, I sprinkle on flaxseed oil (I use it on almost everything) or a delicious homemade sauce for flavour. When time is tight or the vegetables are especially flavoursome, I enjoy them with just a few spices and/or herbs.

Cooking in your household

Every situation calls for a different solution, depending on your household composition. My husband, for example, goes through phases where he eats what I'm eating but at other times craves meat. In your family you may have kids who don't want to change their eating habits and follow the OMS guidelines, so you will need to juggle meals.

Most family members will understand why you are changing your eating habits and support you. Try to find recipes and snacks that all of you can eat and enjoy. Many of the soups, salads and pasta dishes in this book can be your OMS main meal but a side dish for the rest of your family. It is a great way to get everyone to eat healthy food.

Cooking together can become a fun family event. I believe the earlier kids are exposed to healthy eating and the enjoyment of making their own meal, the more likely they are to make healthy food choices when they get older. As Dr Swank writes in his book, encourage the entire family to follow the Swank diet because not only is it easier to cook one meal but also the kids are less likely to develop MS themselves.

Furthermore, many meals can be made the OMS way by changing or omitting only one or two ingredients. If you like pizza and burrito (with an OMS-friendly wrap), replace the meat and cheese with vegetables, tuna, anchovies, tofu and beans. Other dishes such as pasta, risotto or stews can be made the OMS way and, if a family member wants meat to be added, it can be served on the side. The more you cook the OMS way, the more your family members will embrace the life change and find dishes they like, making the cooking process easier and less time consuming, so that everyone is happy and can enjoy their meal together.

One of the biggest challenges in our busy lives is finding the time to prepare these healthy meals. Making double or even triple batches is a huge time saver and means that when you are rushing out the door in the mornings or do not have the time or energy to prepare a meal in the evenings there is always something on hand in the refrigerator or freezer. And if you have OMS leftovers, once or twice a week you could focus on preparing a meat dish for other family members. That way, you only prepare one meal a day or, even better, every other day.

Eating out

Once I had the cooking organised at home, I needed to figure out what to eat when I was out. Packing meals for lunch and having snacks on hand were essential for helping me to get through the day. But I wanted to have a normal social life and be able to eat out in cafes and restaurants too. It took a lot of courage for me to be the 'difficult' customer and ask about the ingredients in dishes and, if necessary, request replacements. I still don't like being 'that' person; however, I am now better at picking the right cafes and restaurants and asking for what I need. An option is to call the restaurant ahead and let them know about your dietary restrictions so they have a chance to get creative and cook something delicious for you before they get busy.

How to reinvent your day with meals

When I switched to the OMS diet, I was hungry all the time. Three plant-based meals a day were not enough fuel to keep me going. This resulted in me eating a lot of bread, which is clearly neither nutritious nor satisfying. And I missed having sweet treats. I had to come up with ideas for food that was readily available and also satisfied me.

That was when I started experimenting and making vegan treats for myself, so that I always had emergency food at home or at work to snack on.

The next revelation was as simple as vegetable crudités and nuts. Even though we shouldn't eat too many nuts a day, they are a great snack to carry with you. Put them in a snap-lock bag or sealed container and off you go. Eating a small serving (30 g/1 oz) of almonds is healthy and satiating, and has helped me to get over that mid-afternoon hump many times. I have also managed to find some OMS-friendly organic granola bars that are made from nuts, seeds and dried fruits. When buying store-bought snacks like these, always read the label carefully and check that they are low in saturated fat and sugar and are relatively unprocessed.

Another great snack idea is a sandwich made with wholegrain, wholemeal (whole-wheat) or sourdough bread, hummus or avocado (or a homemade spread) and sliced vegetables. A classic American PBJ (peanut butter and jelly) sandwich can be made with almond butter instead of peanut butter and with good-quality jam instead of the less healthy sugar-laden jelly. In addition, in this book you will find recipes for 'on the go', such as Ingrid's Energy Bites (see page 55), Pesto Almonds (page 51) or Olive Oil Crackers (page 54) and more.

Things to eat at work

When I started on the OMS diet I had salad (just vegetables, no protein) almost every day for lunch. I am not joking; I didn't know what else to take to work. With the recipes in this book, you'll be better equipped to make filling and nutrient-dense meal choices. Salads, soups, sandwiches and leftovers from the night before are ideal choices for lunch.

What and where to eat out

Eating out was very scary for me in the beginning and it took a long time for me to feel comfortable doing it. Here are some of the cuisines and meals that I have found best suit the OMS lifestyle. Sometimes I ask for ingredients to be omitted or replaced, or to be steamed instead of fried. In my experience it is usually no problem; it's just important to let the waiter know that you have dietary restrictions for health reasons.

I remember reading in Dr Swank's book that he recommends eating out no more than once a week, as there is a risk of possibly consuming unwanted hidden ingredients or heated oil. So, even though it is possible to enjoy a meal out, it is your responsibility to be aware that the food you are eating may not completely comply with OMS guidelines. With all of these cuisines, you will always need to double and triple check that in fact a specific dish in a specific restaurant is OMS-safe.

African

Ethiopian food has a lot of vegan options that I've found suitable. They consist of vegetables and beans, which are scooped up with a teff tortilla (teff is a grain used in traditional Ethiopian cuisine).

Caution: Always check the type and amount of oil used.

Asian

Chinese food is known to be very oily. In my experience in the US and in larger cities in Europe, Chinese, Korean, Thai and Vietnamese restaurants typically have steamed vegetables, tofu and prawns (shrimp) with rice on the menu. I find that many Asian restaurants also offer some steamed options, or will make them specially for you. Don't be afraid to ask. Furthermore, many Asian cuisines have soups (like ramen or pho) with vegetables, seafood and tofu plus rice or soba noodles. Check that the broth is 100 per cent vegetarian or fish based, as many Asian broths are based on chicken or beef stock. Salads, such as papaya salad and seaweed salad, are good options too.

Fine dining

Business lunches and dinners are often held at high-end restaurants. They mostly have salmon (if nothing else) they will steam for you. When you make your request, I suggest stressing that they use no oil (I have often had oil drizzled over my steamed fish, even though I asked for none). In recent years, vegan soups and main meals have become available but you often have to be careful about the amount of nuts or replacement products they use (such as vegan cheese, vegan sour cream, etc.). Salads with tuna or prawns (shrimp), such as a niçoise (without the egg), are often served in such restaurants. In most cases grilled (broiled) fish is also fine.

Italian

At an Italian restaurant you can always find a salmon or white fish dish that you can ask to be steamed and served with a salad without dressing, steamed vegetables or pasta. Extra virgin olive oil (or flaxseed oil brought from home) can be drizzled over the top. Italian restaurants almost always have pasta with plain tomato sauce, often with vegetables and prawns (shrimp). Always make sure the tomato sauce is made without butter or cheese.

Another favourite option of mine is pizza, made without cheese. Topping options include tomato sauce with herbs, anchovies, tuna and vegetables. A nice Italian restaurant will most likely make risotto for you dairy-free but remember it will take a good 20 minutes so be prepared for the wait. They may also only make it for a minimum of two people. A fish-style risotto is a good option in a decent Italian restaurant as Italians generally don't serve seafood with cheese.

Caution: If you have pasta, make sure it is not pre-cooked and stored in oil or butter. Always double-check that dishes don't have dairy—for example, parmesan or butter—in the tomato sauce.

Japanese

I love Japanese food, especially sashimi and sushi, and it is very OMS-friendly. Options include classic rolls with fish or vegetables, miso and clear fish soups, ramen and seaweed salads.

Caution: Be careful with rolls that include tempura (fried battered vegetables and fish/seafood) or mayonnaise (often called spicy rolls, such as spicy tuna, spicy salmon rolls).

Mexican

At first I avoided Mexican restaurants, as everything seemed to be made with cheese, meat and wheat tortillas (which are not OMS-friendly due to vegetable oil). However, I realised that I could have corn tortillas, as they are usually fat-free (having said that, I always double-check). Vegetable burritos without sour cream and cheese are always an option. And a good starter—which may also be eaten as a main—is ceviche, which is cured fish. It's very OMS-suitable. Guacamole with bread is good too. Rice and beans with salad or steamed vegetables are fine for a main meal, as long as the beans are not refried.

Caution: If you are sensitive to omega-6, be careful when eating Mexican food, as a meal that consists of a tortilla with rice, beans and guacamole may be very high in omega-6. Bring a flask of flaxseed oil (best frozen when you leave the house) to balance it out with some omega-3. For more information on omega-6, see *Overcoming Multiple Sclerosis*, 2nd edition, Step 1. In addition, always check on the ingredients of guacamole when you're eating out. If pre-packaged guacamole is served it will probably contain non-OMS-friendly ingredients.

Middle Eastern

Middle Eastern cuisine features some wonderful dips and salads, such as hummus, baba ghanoush, tabouleh, vegetarian-stuffed grape leaves and vegetable dishes cooked with olive oil. But they also use dairy products, such as yoghurt, so I always double-check the ingredients in a dish.

Vegetarian/vegan

I find vegetarian and vegan restaurants great yet challenging at the same time. They have many delicious dishes I crave but they are often made with a lot of oil or replacement products that I can't eat. On the other hand, very plain dishes, which consist of whole grains, legumes and vegetables, can be a really healthy and safe option. Salads that have some added protein, such as tofu, beans and grains, make nutritious and satisfying main meals.

Eating out at other people's houses

Eating at somebody else's house can be an emotional challenge. What do you do when you haven't shared your diagnosis but you don't want to upset the host? I used to just say that for health reasons I eat vegan plus fish but would then watch carefully to make sure that not too much oil was used in the dish.

If it's just drinks, one solution is to eat before the event. Others are to suggest some dishes you can eat, or offer to bring one or two OMS-friendly options you and the other guests can enjoy. When I bring food to parties, my go-to option is hummus with vegetables or bread. Guacamole, crudités or smoked salmon also work well. Another good solution is to invite people to your house so you can cook OMS-friendly food.

If it's for lunch or dinner, again, offer to bring a dish or two. Ratatouille, vegetable couscous and vegan-mashed potatoes are just a few options that work well with meat and other main course dishes.

Dealing with other dietary restrictions

Following the OMS diet and being vegan, vegetarian or gluten-free can make cooking and eating out even more difficult. This cookbook mainly focuses on the OMS diet; however, many recipes are vegan and gluten-free, or can be easily adapted—for example, by replacing egg white with the flax egg (see page 31). Many people trying to follow an ultra-healthy diet prefer to refrain from eating sugar even though sugar in small quantities is permitted on the OMS diet. Some of the desserts contain sugar and others do not. The OMS diet is a plant-based wholefood diet, which means we should consume food in its natural state or as close to that as possible. So, a good mix of raw and cooked vegetables, fresh fruit and raw nuts (in moderation) will be beneficial for everyone. Ingredients like sugar and flour should be used and consumed sparingly, but using them occasionally, as in some of the dessert recipes in this book, is not problematic.

Flaxseed oil and flaxseeds

Flaxseeds and flaxseed oil deserve their own chapter because they are such an important part of the OMS diet. Some people take shots or spoonfuls of flaxseed oil all in one hit (1–2 tablespoons per day), while others add it to their food or mix it with juice. Some do a combination of the two. If you are travelling and cannot refrigerate the oil, then a supplement in capsule form is the best way to get your daily dose of omega-3. If you are gone just for a few days, you could grind up some flaxseeds and bring flaxseed meal on your trip (the nutrients and omega-3 are only safe for a couple of days). Alternatively, you can take your coffee grinder with you and use it to grind the flaxseeds.

Adding flaxseed meal to your muesli and other dishes is another great way to increase your intake of omega-3. Remember: the flaxseeds have to be ground so the body can absorb the fat (otherwise they travel undigested through your digestive tract).

Flaxseed oil is very high in omega-3 and is very unstable. Therefore it quickly becomes rancid if it is not stored in the fridge. The oil should not be heated under any circumstances (even at a low temperature). If flaxseed oil is desired for a dish, then the most suitable OMS way to add it is to prepare the dish without any oil then drizzle on a little flaxseed oil after cooking. If you find flaxseed oil palatable, adding it to salads, vegetables, grains, legumes, fish and breakfast options, such as pancakes, yoghurt and muesli, is a great solution.

Flaxseeds and freshly ground flaxseed meal can be added to many dishes. Besides omega-3, their many nutritional benefits include dietary fibre, manganese and vitamin B1. They are also used to improve digestive health, relieve constipation and lower cholesterol. So flaxseeds have many health benefits besides omega-3, which is so essential for those on the OMS diet; however, it is important to remember that for omega-3 intake, flaxseed oil is better than either flaxseed or flaxseed meal.

Abbreviations

Chia egg   1 tablespoon chia seeds and 2 tablespoons water

Flax egg   1 tablespoon flaxseeds and 2 tablespoons water

OMS   Overcoming Multiple Sclerosis (the program, the lifestyle of eating and cooking)

OMS-friendly Food we eat following the diet in the OMS program

OMS MENU PLAN

Sandra Perry

This is a suggested menu plan for a week, using recipes from this book. Each day offers a selection of dishes which represent a balanced nutritional intake on the OMS diet.

	MONDAY	TUESDAY	WEDNESDAY	THURSDAY	FRIDAY	SATURDAY	SUNDAY
BREAKFAST	Granola 43	Tropical chia breakfast bowl 42	Scrambled tofu 40	Kousmine-Budwig breakfast 36	Overnight oatmeal 44	Breakfast burrito 41	Apple quinoa breakfast 37
SNACK (optional)	Savoury popped pumpkin seeds 57	Ingrid's energy bites (2) 55	Pesto almonds 51 and one piece of fruit	Pita chips 56 with Spinach dip 69	Peppermint bar 52	Quinoa blueberry muffin 235	Pita chips 56 with Baba ghanoush 64
LUNCH	Vegan split pea and sweet potato soup 111	Tuna and cannellini bean salad 80	Chickpea salad with mint 82	Fish soup 101	Quinoa detox salad 86	Vietnamese summer rolls 73	Haricot bean and watercress soup 103
SNACK (optional)	Ingrid's energy bites (2) 55	Pita chips 56 with Baba ghanoush 64	Baked fruit and nut clusters (2) 53	Peppermint bar 52	Pita chips 56 with Spinach dip 69	Savoury popped pumpkin seeds 57	Quinoa blueberry muffin 235
DINNER	Chilli and tomato fish 141 with Rice with kale 212	Vegan shepherd's pie 118	Salmon kedgeree 134 with Steamed brussels sprouts and tahini dill sauce 202	Potato quinoa patties with chickpea curry 149	Vietnamese stir-fry 188	Lentil-mushroom burger 168 with Crispy oven fries 205	Fish tacos 146

ADVICE FROM A NUTRITIONIST

Sandra Perry

Definition of a wholefood diet

On the OMS Recovery Program, eating a wholefood diet is strongly recommended. A wholefood diet is essentially eating foods that are unprocessed or unrefined and therefore are as close to their natural state or form as possible. Processing and refining foods not only strips vital nutrients, such as vitamins, minerals and fibre, but also adds fat, sugar, salt and preservatives.

Sourcing food

Vegetables

Buying locally grown fruit and vegetables in season will help keep your costs down, as imported fruits and vegetables are often expensive and chemically treated to allow for transport between countries. Eating seasonally ensures that your diet is constantly changing, which provides variety and avoids overexposure to the same fruits and vegetables.

It is well known that commercial produce is exposed to high levels of pesticides and herbicides. Therefore, reducing your exposure to these toxins by buying biodynamic and organic produce makes sense if your budget allows and you are satisfied with your country's organic food regulations. Local farmers' markets often provide good quality organic produce at reasonable prices.

Consider starting a vegetable garden at home. If space is limited, just use pots to grow a selection of leafy greens, herbs and cherry tomatoes.

All fruits and vegetables should be washed well before using. You will find a number of recipes on the internet using various combinations of vinegar, salt and baking soda to make a natural fruit and vegetable wash.

Fish

Choose fish and seafood that is fished or harvested sustainably from unpolluted water sources. Where possible, consume smaller ocean fish, such as sardines, as the mercury content is likely to be lower than in the larger predatory fish that feed on them.

Food allergies and intolerances

Managing food allergies and intolerances while following the OMS recommendations shouldn't be difficult.

The eight most common food allergens are milk, egg, wheat, soy, peanuts, tree nuts, fish and shellfish.

As dairy products are to be avoided in the OMS diet, milk allergies will not be an issue.

Gluten (wheat, barley, oats, rye) allergies/intolerances can be managed by replacing wheat with the large number of gluten-free grains available.

Egg, soy, peanuts, tree nuts, fish and shellfish allergies can be managed by avoiding the offending products.

Although processed foods are discouraged, some may wish to occasionally use minimally processed OMS-friendly products. Food manufacturers are required by law to list the most common allergens on product labels, so carefully reading the labels will ensure that you avoid consuming allergenic foods.

If you have the challenge of a combination of allergies and are unsure if you are getting enough variety and nutrients in your diet, consult a registered nutritionist for advice.

Pregnancy

The OMS nutrient-rich wholefood diet provides plenty of scope and variety to support a healthy pregnancy. Eating frequent, smaller meals can be helpful if morning sickness or heartburn are problematic. Avoid seafood, as this is not recommended during pregnancy. If you have any concerns regarding your dietary intake during pregnancy, consult a registered nutritionist for advice.

BREAKFAST

Kousmine-Budwig breakfast
Catherine Lamontagne, Chicoutimi, Canada
Serves 1

4 tablespoons silken tofu or soy yoghurt

2 tablespoons flaxseed oil

2 tablespoons freshly ground flaxseeds or 6 almonds or 6 hazelnuts or any other
  type of nut, excluding peanuts

1 small banana, mashed, or 2 teaspoons honey

juice of ½ lemon

2 tablespoons freshly ground wholegrain cereals such as wheat, rice, millet,
  buckwheat or oats

½ cup seasonal fresh fruit (such as strawberries, raspberries, cherries,
  grapes, chopped apple)

Place the tofu or soy yoghurt and flaxseed oil in a bowl and mix with a fork until
you obtain a rich, white and creamy blend. Add the remaining ingredients and
mix well.

NOTE FROM CATHERINE LAMONTAGNE: This recipe comes from Dr
Catherine Kousmine, 1904–1992, who was a renowned dietitian, researcher
and independent thinker. A contemporary of Dr Swank, she lived and worked
in Europe but was very well known in Quebec, where it was all the rage in the
1980s and 1990s to start the day with her famous recipe. She used it as a basic
building block in her diet and healing program, 'La Crème Budwig', after her
friend Johanna Budwig, a German biochemist. For the grains, Dr Kousmine
recommended freshly ground wholegrain cereals. In Quebec, followers of 'La
Crème Budwig' typically keep a coffee grinder just for this.

Apart from being a rich source of calcium, iron and zinc, this breakfast is rich
in linolenic acid (healthy fats) and provides substantial levels of vitamins and
minerals. The combination of these ingredients makes this recipe particularly
efficient.

Apple quinoa breakfast

Ingrid Adelsberger, Los Angeles, United States

Serves 2

½ cup quinoa, rinsed well

¾ cup water

½ teaspoon cinnamon, plus extra for sprinkling

1 teaspoon vanilla extract

¼ cup unsweetened applesauce (optional)

2 tablespoons sultanas

½ cup warmed plant-based milk (I prefer almond)

½ pink lady apple, diced

2 tablespoons walnuts, chopped

Combine the quinoa, water, cinnamon and vanilla in a small saucepan and bring to the boil. Reduce to a simmer, cover then cook until you can fluff the quinoa with a fork, 15 minutes.

Stir in the apple sauce and the sultanas, then pour in the warmed plant-based milk. Divide the quinoa mixture between two bowls, top with the apple and walnuts and sprinkle with cinnamon.

Oat-flour crepes

Bryony Forde, Lower Hutt, New Zealand

Serves 2–3

1 cup rolled (porridge) oats
1 cup wholemeal (whole-wheat) or plain (all-purpose) flour
1 teaspoon baking powder
2 cups (ish) soy milk
2 tablespoons (ish) honey
strawberries, blueberries and maple syrup, to serve

Place the rolled oats in a food processor and whiz until a flour forms. Combine all the ingredients in a food processor and process until a batter forms; adjust to get the consistency of a pourable but not too thin batter.

Heat a little bit of water in a non-stick frying pan over medium heat. Pour on some of the batter and tip the pan to ensure it covers the base. Turn down the heat to low. Watch carefully: when bubbles form and then start to pop on the surface, it's time to turn the crepe over. Cook for a couple of minutes until golden. Take off the heat and eat immediately or place on a warmed plate in a very low oven to keep warm while you finish cooking all the crepes, so you can sit and share a weekend brunch. (The more you cook, the faster they'll be ready once your pan gets up to, and maintains, its heat.)

Top with whatever you fancy. In our house we enjoy the crepes with sliced strawberries, some blueberries and a wee bit of maple syrup.

Blueberry pancakes

Judit Gulyás, Debrecen, Hungary

Gluten-free • Makes 7 pancakes

1 tablespoon extra virgin olive oil

1½ cups gluten-free flour (we use 95 per cent millet flour with a 5 per cent freshly ground flaxseed and poppy seed mixture)

1 teaspoon baking powder

1 teaspoon baking soda

½ cup ground poppy seeds

1 cup almond or rice milk

1–2 tablespoons unrefined sugar, coconut sugar or other sweetener

1½ cups blueberries

Mix the olive oil, flour, baking powder, baking soda, ground poppy seeds, almond or rice milk and sweetener until you get a nice, thick batter. Add ¾ cup of blueberries.

Heat a non-stick frying pan over medium heat and add a bit of water. Use one ladle of batter for each pancake and cook until the top is blistered and the underside is a nice golden brown. Turn the pancake over and cook the other side until it is also golden brown. Repeat until all the batter is used, keeping the finished pancakes warm in a low oven.

Tip the remaining blueberries into a non-stick saucepan and cook over medium heat until a jam-like texture is reached.

Serve the pancakes with the warm blueberry sauce.

Scrambled tofu

Sandra Perry, Auckland, New Zealand

Gluten-free • Serves 4

3 garlic cloves, chopped
5 cm piece of ginger, sliced
1 teaspoon black mustard seeds
1 teaspoon ground turmeric
500 g (1 lb 2 oz) firm tofu
4 spring onions (scallions), roughly chopped
4 large handfuls of English spinach, stems removed, leaves chopped
2 tablespoons tamari or soy sauce
2 tablespoons mirin
toasted sesame seeds, to serve
chopped fresh herbs, to serve

In a heavy-based non-stick frying pan, add the garlic, ginger, mustard seeds and turmeric and sauté gently over medium heat, stirring occasionally, until fragrant. Add a little water to prevent sticking and burning.

Crumble the tofu into the pan, stirring to combine all the ingredients well. Add the spring onion and spinach, stir again, and continue to cook until the spinach wilts. Pour in the tamari or soy sauce and mirin and cook for about 10 minutes until all the flavours have melded, the greens are pleasantly tender and the tofu is cooked through.

Spoon the scrambled tofu onto 4 plates and top with some toasted sesame seeds and chopped herbs.

Breakfast burrito

Ingrid Adelsberger, Los Angeles, United States
Gluten-free • Serves 3–4

100 g (3½ oz) extra-firm tofu, rinsed,
  or 4 egg whites
½ onion, finely chopped
2 garlic cloves, finely chopped
1 small potato or sweet potato, cut into
  2.5 cm (1 inch) cubes (optional)
½ green or red capsicum (bell pepper),
  chopped, or 6–8 cremini or button
  mushrooms, thinly sliced
½ cup fresh or frozen corn kernels
½ cup cooked long-grain brown rice

½ cup cooked beans (I prefer black)
sea salt and freshly ground black pepper
½ teaspoon chilli powder
1 cup salsa (homemade—for a recipe,
  see page 231)
8 small or 4 large corn tortillas
1 avocado, sliced
½ cup soy yoghurt
finely chopped coriander (cilantro),
  to serve
1–2 tablespoons lime juice

Press out as much water as you can from the tofu, then chop and set aside.

Cook the onion in a large, heavy-based frying pan over medium heat until it turns translucent. Make sure to add a bit of water if the onion begins to stick too much and take on colour. Add the garlic and cook, stirring, for another 2–3 minutes.

Add the potato or sweet potato and cook, stirring occasionally, for about 15 minutes until a fork easily pierces the potato or sweet potato. (Alternatively, you could boil the potato or sweet potato until tender and add it with the other vegetables and skip this step.)

Stir in the capsicum or mushrooms, corn, rice, beans, salt, pepper and chilli powder and cook for 7–10 minutes until the vegetables are softened. Add the salsa and tofu, or egg whites (if using), and cook, gently stirring, for 1–2 minutes until heated through.

Warm the tortillas in a frying pan, or in the microwave for 30 seconds. Divide the mixture between the tortillas, add some avocado, spoon on some soy yoghurt and top with a sprinkle of coriander and a squeeze of lime juice.

NOTE: You probably have most of these ingredients in your fridge and pantry but, if not, try substituting some of the ingredients with what you do have.

Tropical chia breakfast bowl

Vicky, United States

Serves 4

1 cup chia seeds

2 cups coconut water

1 cup your favourite tropical fruit (such as papaya, mango, etc.), cubed

2 tablespoons your favourite nuts (such as walnuts, almonds, hazelnuts, etc.), crushed

2 tablespoons your favourite cereal, rolled (porridge) oats or muesli

1 tablespoon flaxseeds (whole, ground or oil)

Place the chia seeds and coconut water in a large bowl and set aside to soak until thick and sticky, at least 15 minutes.

Mix the remaining ingredients into the chia seed mixture and serve.

Granola

Wendy Wood, Murchison, New Zealand

Makes 16 portions

10 handfuls of whole rolled (porridge) oats

1 handful of nuts (I like a mixture of whole almonds and chopped hazelnuts)

2 handfuls of dried fruit (I like a mixture of cranberries, chopped dates and apricots)

1 heaped tablespoon ground cinnamon, or more to taste

Mix everything together and store in an airtight container for 1 month, or in the freezer for 3 months.

TIP: Serve the granola with your favourite plant-based milk or fruit juice to loosen. Alternatively, serve with soy yoghurt and fresh or stewed fruit and a drizzle of honey.

Overnight oatmeal

Ruth Johnson, Onkaparinga Hills, Australia

Serves 1

½ apple
¼ teaspoon ground cinnamon
1 teaspoon honey
¼–½ cup rolled (porridge) oats
rice milk (or preferred plant-based milk), to cover
2 teaspoons any seeds and/or chopped nuts (optional)
2 teaspoons flaxseed oil (optional)

Grate the apple into a bowl and sprinkle on the cinnamon. Drizzle the honey over the grated apple and add the rolled oats. Cover generously with the milk and place in the fridge overnight.

In the morning, add the seeds, nuts and flaxseed oil (if using). Stir and eat.

 For a sweet breakfast treat, add maple syrup to warm hemp milk and oats, and sprinkle with flaxseeds and sunflower seeds.

Kathryn Hughes, Wiltshire, United Kingdom

Breakfast bars

Anne Sullivan, Worcester, United Kingdom
Makes 10–12

2 tablespoons flaxseed meal
½ cup warm water
175 g (6 oz) rolled (porridge) oats
115 g (4 oz) quinoa, rinsed
2 tablespoons chia seeds
1 teaspoon baking powder
½ teaspoon freshly grated nutmeg
2 tablespoons honey
3 bananas, mashed
1 teaspoon vanilla extract
55 g (2 oz) walnuts or pecans, finely crushed
55 g (2 oz) chopped dates (or whatever dried fruit you like)
55 g (2 oz) raisins

Preheat the oven to 190°C (375°F/gas 5). Line a 20 cm (8 inch) square baking tin with baking paper.

Mix the flaxseed meal and water in a bowl and leave for 5 minutes.

In a separate bowl, combine the oats, quinoa, chia seeds, baking powder, nutmeg and honey. Mix in the banana, vanilla and flaxseed mixture. Fold in the nuts and dried fruit and stir well. Press with your hands into the prepared tin (the mixture will be soft) and bake for 25–30 minutes until it turns a light golden colour. Allow to cool in the tin before turning out and cutting into slices.

These bars keep well stored in an airtight tin for up to a week. Fantastic for breakfast or crumbled over fruit. Enjoy!

Egg white omelette

Ingrid Adelsberger, Los Angeles, United States

Serves 2

1 small onion, finely chopped

1 garlic clove, minced

12 cherry tomatoes, finely chopped
(about ½ cup)

about 4 handfuls of fresh spinach
(or frozen spinach, thawed, with
excess water squeezed out)

3 mushrooms, finely chopped
(eg shiitake, portabello)

8 egg whites

1–2 tablespoons water

salt and freshly ground black pepper,
to taste

few drops extra virgin olive oil

¼ teaspoon crushed pepper

1 teaspoon flaxseed oil (optional)

Add the onion, garlic, tomatoes, spinach, mushrooms and a pinch of salt (optional) into a small non-stick pan. Add about 1 tablespoon of water if necessary and cook, stirring, until the onion is soft, about 4–5 minutes. Transfer the spinach mixture to a bowl, cover and keep warm.

In a medium bowl, whisk the egg whites, water and a pinch of salt and pepper until frothy. Gently heat a medium non-stick pan over low heat, then brush it with the extra virgin olive oil. Add half the egg whites, swirling them to evenly cover the bottom of the pan. As you are cooking the omelette over a very low temperature, you may need to cover the pan so the egg whites can cook through. Cook until set, about 3–5 minutes, so you'll be able to peel off the edge and fold it.

Spoon half the spinach mixture onto half the omelette, fold it over and cook for another minute, then slide the omelette onto a serving plate. Repeat with the remaining egg whites and spinach mixture. Top with crushed pepper and drizzle with flaxseed oil (if using).

NOTE: To stop the egg whites sticking to the pan, and ending up with scrambled egg whites instead of an omelette, it's okay to use a bit of oil. As egg whites are 75 per cent water and you are cooking them over a very low heat, the pan will not reach a temperature that damages the oil.

VARIATIONS: You can use any vegetables you like. Smoked salmon with dill is also delicious.

If you have children and want to shift the whole family to the OMS diet, take your time. Every family has its own favourite recipes. When you suddenly stop eating them all, you don't have a happy family. In the beginning, I cooked OMS meals for the whole family on some days and on other days two different things. After a while the 'family-favourite repertoire' included more and more OMS recipes. So now the whole family eats OMS most days. This saves a lot of time, is healthy and everyone is happy. After some time, the children really forget their former favourite recipes and have new OMS-friendly favourites.

Hester Dekker, Vught, The Netherlands

SNACKS
AND
ENERGY
BARS

Salty sesame biscuits (triangolini)

Hester Dekker, Vught, The Netherlands

Makes about 85 little triangles

125 g (4½ oz) plain (all-purpose) flour, plus extra if needed
½ teaspoon baking powder
2 tablespoons sesame seeds, plus extra to sprinkle on top
1 tablespoon poppy seeds
1 teaspoon sea salt, plus extra to sprinkle on top
pinch of sugar
1 tablespoon extra virgin olive oil
75 ml (2¼ fl oz) water, plus extra if needed

Preheat the oven to 200°C (400°F/gas 6). Line a baking tray with baking paper.

Sift the flour and baking powder into a large bowl. Add the sesame seeds, poppy seeds, salt and sugar and mix well. Add the olive oil and water and stir with a fork until everything sticks together.

Knead the mixture for a few minutes until you have a smooth dough. Add some flour if it is too sticky, or some water if it is too dry. Place between two sheets of baking paper and roll out to form a 30 cm (12 inch) square. Cut into 3 cm (1¼ inch) wide strips and place on the prepared tray. Cut the strips into triangles, spray with water (in a spray bottle) and sprinkle on some extra salt and sesame seeds. Bake for 8–10 minutes until lightly coloured and crunchy.

NOTE: These biscuits can be kept in an airtight container for up to 1 week.

Pesto almonds

Andree, Dromana, Australia

Gluten-free • Makes 25 snack portions

1 bunch of basil
4 large garlic cloves, peeled
1 teaspoon Himalayan salt or sea salt, plus extra to sprinkle
2 cups flaked or chopped almonds
4 tablespoons extra virgin olive oil

Preheat the oven to 150°C (300°F/gas 2). Line two baking trays with baking paper.

Wash and air dry the basil leaves. Arrange the basil leaves evenly on the prepared trays and place in the oven to dry for 5–10 minutes. Watch closely, to ensure the leaves don't burn. Let the basil cool, then crumble into a bowl and set aside. (Alternatively, use store-bought dried basil.)

Mash the garlic and salt with a fork.

Spread the almonds evenly over two baking trays, evenly sprinkle the garlic on top and then the basil. Season with salt and drizzle 2 tablespoons of olive oil over each tray of almonds. Using two forks, turn the almonds over until all the ingredients are well mixed. Bake for 10–15 minutes; keep checking to make sure they are no more than slightly golden brown around the edges. Let cool and store in an airtight container for 1 month.

 NOTE: You can also dry the basil in the microwave.

Peppermint bars

Ingrid Adelsberger, Los Angeles, United States

Makes 12 bars

2 cups rolled (porridge) oats, plus 3 tablespoons extra

3 tablespoons almonds

3 tablespoons walnuts

2–3 tablespoons cacao powder

pinch of sea salt

2 heaped tablespoons packed soft brown sugar

100 ml (3½ fl oz) maple syrup

2–3 tablespoons almond milk

1 teaspoon peppermint extract

1 tablespoon extra virgin olive oil

Line a 20 cm (8 inch) square baking tin with baking paper.

Place the rolled oats in a food processor and whiz until a flour forms. Set aside.

Again, in the food processor, add the almonds and walnuts and process to a very fine crumble. Add the oat flour, 2 tablespoons of cacao powder, the salt and brown sugar and process until combined. Pour in the maple syrup, almond milk, peppermint extract and extra virgin olive oil and pulse until a ball forms. Add another tablespoon of cacao powder, if desired, and the extra rolled oats and pulse until combined.

Tip the mixture (it will be very sticky) into the prepared tin. Now take a second piece of baking paper and place it on top (because the dough is so sticky) and press down evenly with your fingers to smooth it out. Place in the freezer for 15 minutes, then cut into squares. Store in an airtight container in the freezer for up to 2 weeks.

Baked fruit and nut clusters

Hester Dekker, Vught, The Netherlands

Makes about 20–25 clusters

3 egg whites

300 g (10½ oz) mixed berries (such as raspberries, blueberries, mulberries, etc.), chopped

¾ cup mixed seeds (chia seeds, flaxseeds, pumpkin seeds [pepitas], sunflower seeds, hemp seeds, etc.)

⅓ cup sugar

4 handfuls of mixed nuts (such as almonds, hazelnuts, walnuts)

Preheat the oven to 180°C (350°F/gas 4). Line a baking tray with baking paper.

Beat the egg whites with an electric mixer until stiff peaks form.

Add the remaining ingredients to the egg whites and fold in. Spoon little heaps of the mixture onto the prepared tray and bake for about 20 minutes until they darken in colour.

NOTE: These cookies don't get hard, they stay soft. Fresh or frozen berries can be used.

Olive oil crackers

Leanne Shearer, Berwick, Australia

Makes 60 cookies

2¼ cups plain (all-purpose) flour
½ cup warm water
3 tablespoons olive oil
1 teaspoon Herbamare (see note) or other seasoning of choice or sea salt, plus extra
1–2 tablespoons soy milk

Preheat the oven to 180°C (350°F/gas 4).

Place the flour, water, olive oil and seasoning in a food processor and process until small balls form. The mixture will look like pebbles. Remove and knead to form a ball.

Divide the dough into two balls. Roll out each ball thinly on some baking paper (the thinner the dough, the crispier the crackers will be), cut into rectangles, then transfer the paper and crackers to a baking tray. Brush the crackers with the soy milk and sprinkle with the extra seasoning. Bake for 15 minutes. Place the crackers on a wire rack to cool. Store in an airtight container for up to 2 weeks.

NOTE: Herbamare is a seasoning that combines dried herbs and vegetables with sea salt.

Ingrid's energy bites

Ingrid Adelsberger, Los Angeles, United States

Makes 16 balls

¾ cup almonds

¾ cup lightly packed pitted Medjool dates

3 tablespoons dried apricots

3 tablespoons rolled (porridge) oats (optional)

1 teaspoon cacao powder

3 tablespoons hazelnuts

1–2 pinches of fine sea salt

In a food processor, process the almonds until roughly chopped. It's okay if some bigger pieces remain. Do not process for too long, as you do not want to end up with almond meal. Remove ⅓ cup of processed almonds and set aside.

Add the dates, dried apricots, rolled oats (if using) and cacao powder to the food processor and process until finely chopped and sticky. You may need to stop and scrape down the side of the bowl a few times. Add the hazelnuts and pulse until chopped. Add salt to taste and pulse. Finally, pulse in the reserved almonds. If the dough is too dry to roll into a ball, add water, a teaspoon at a time, until the dough comes together.

Roll the dough into bite-sized balls with wet hands. Store in an airtight container in the fridge for 2–3 weeks.

TIP: These treats have been my lifesaver over the past few years. When I'm out and people eat something sweet that I can't have, I will have one of these (from the stash hidden in my purse).

VARIATION: Try making these bites with dried cherries and walnuts instead of the apricots and hazelnuts.

Pita chips

Lucie Williams, Paraparaumu, New Zealand

Serves 4–6

5 small pita bread rounds
1½ tablespoons extra virgin olive oil
pinch of sea salt

Preheat the oven to 150°C (300°F/gas 2).

Very lightly brush each pita flat bread round with the extra virgin olive oil, sprinkle on the salt and cut into four strips. Cut each strip into bite-sized pieces and place on a baking tray. Bake for about 20 minutes until golden. Let cool before serving with your favourite dip.

TIP: Prepare these chips in batches (two or three packets of pita bread at a time). They keep very well in an airtight container for 2 weeks.

Savoury popped pumpkin seeds

Claire Donkin, Ballsgate Cottage, United Kingdom

Serves 1

2 tablespoons pumpkin seeds (pepitas)
2 teaspoons tamari or soy sauce, or to taste

Warm a heavy-based frying pan over medium heat. Add the pumpkin seeds and keep them moving in the pan until they start to pop. Once the majority of the seeds have popped, add the tamari or soy sauce. Move the seeds around in the evaporating tamari or soy sauce, so they are all covered in some of the sticky coating. Allow to cool, then munch happily.

We have turned a top drawer, which is easily accessed in the kitchen, into an OMS snack drawer. It contains sunflower and pumpkin seeds (pepitas), nuts, raisins, dried apricots, dates and rice cakes. And we keep fresh juices on the top shelf in the fridge. These small changes help us to focus on OMS things when we are hungry.

Claes Nermark, Helsingborg, Sweden

Almond butter and goji berry flapjacks

Jamie Smith, Hampshire, United Kingdom

Makes 15–20

100 ml (3½ fl oz) golden syrup (light treacle) (I sometimes use 110 ml [3¾ fl oz]
  if I top up with a handful of cashews)
¼ cup very lightly packed soft brown sugar
100 g (3½ oz) crunchy almond butter
1 teaspoon vanilla extract
1 large handful of goji berries, or to taste
1½ cups rolled (porridge) oats
75 g (2½ oz) puffed rice cereal

Melt the golden syrup and sugar in a saucepan over medium heat and cook till all the sugar is dissolved. Add the almond butter, vanilla and goji berries. Stir in the combined oats and puffed rice (and cashews, if using) until you have a sticky mixture.

Press into a 30 × 15 cm (12 × 6 inch) baking tin and set aside to cool, then cut up and eat!

NOTES: If you use too much golden syrup, the flapjacks will be quite hard; if the mixture is too dry, they will be crumbly.

In the UK, flapjacks are square bars made with oats, syrup, fat and usually nuts or fruits, but in the US flapjacks are pancakes!

Baked wasabi edamame

Ingrid Adelsberger, Los Angeles, United States

Makes about 2 cups

450 g (1 lb) frozen shelled edamame (green soy beans), thawed
2 teaspoons extra virgin olive oil
1 teaspoon sea salt
½ teaspoon freshly ground black pepper
1 teaspoon wasabi powder

Preheat the oven to 190°C (375°F/gas 5).

Spread the edamame on a clean tea towel (dish towel) and pat gently with another tea towel to dry them as much as possible.

Toss the edamame with the olive oil, salt, pepper and wasabi powder in a bowl. Taste and add more seasoning if desired. Spread the edamame in a single layer on a baking tray and roast, stirring every 10 minutes, for 30–40 minutes until puffed and golden brown. Remove the roasted edamame from the oven and transfer to a serving bowl. They are best eaten within a few hours of roasting.

NOTE: You can make these just with salt and pepper, or add any seasoning you desire.

STARTERS
AND
SALADS

Semi-dried tomato and basil dip

Sandra Perry, Auckland, New Zealand

Serves 2–3

275 g (9¾ oz) firm tofu
½ cup semi-dried tomatoes
1 garlic clove, peeled
juice of ½ lemon
1 tablespoon balsamic vinegar
½ cup basil
sea salt and freshly ground black pepper
vegetable crudités or wholegrain bread and crackers, to serve

Place the first seven ingredients in a food processor or blender and mix until well combined. Transfer to a small bowl, season to taste and serve immediately with crudités or your favourite bread and crackers.

Walnut dukkah

Wendy Wood, Murchison, New Zealand

Gluten-free • Makes 20

1½ cups walnuts
2 teaspoons sesame seeds
1 tablespoon coriander seeds
2 tablespoons cumin seeds
1½ teaspoons fennel seeds
1 teaspoon sea salt
flaxseed oil or extra virgin olive oil, to serve
sourdough or wholegrain bread, cut into cubes, to serve

Preheat the oven to 170°C (325°F/gas 3).

Spread the walnuts on one baking tray and the sesame, coriander, cumin and fennel seeds on another baking tray and roast for about 10 minutes, or until lightly toasted. Cool.

Put the walnuts and seeds into a food processor; add the salt and pulse to form fine crumbs.

Serve the dukkah with the flaxseed or olive oil and cubes of bread for dipping.

NOTE: This recipe makes a jarful and keeps well. Sprinkle the dukkah on your salads, or crumb fish fillets with it before you bake them. You can use whatever nuts you have—almonds and hazelnuts are nice, but rub the skin off the hazelnuts after toasting.

Baba ghanoush

Jack McNulty, Zurich, Switzerland

Gluten-free • Serves 4–6

800 g (1 lb 12 oz) eggplant (aubergine)
150 ml (5 fl oz) water
2 teaspoons sea salt
2 garlic cloves, grated
4 thyme sprigs, leaves picked
juice of 1–2 lemons
2 tablespoons tahini
1½–2 tablespoons olive oil, or to taste

Begin by preparing the eggplant. Peel alternating long strips of the skin vertically on the eggplant. The idea is to keep most of the skin on, which is where the flavour comes from, but to remove just enough to lighten the overall flavour and colour. Slice the eggplant into 2 cm (¾ inch) cubes.

Place the eggplant and water in a pressure cooker along with the salt, garlic, thyme and about 1 tablespoon of lemon juice. Close and lock the lid of the pressure cooker. Bring to high pressure over medium–high heat (that would be the second ring on your pressure cooker), reduce the temperature to maintain the pressure and cook for 8 minutes.

Remove the pressure cooker from the heat, release the pressure quickly by placing it under cold running water. Remove the lid carefully and take out the eggplant and place it in a strainer. Carefully strain away most of the water, making sure to reserve some of it in case you need to thin the dip later.

Place the eggplant, tahini, the remaining lemon juice and 1½ tablespoons of olive oil in a high-speed blender and blend, starting on slow and quickly increasing the speed to maximum, to produce a very smooth and creamy dip. (Alternatively, smash everything together with a fork or purée with a hand-held blender.) Adjust seasoning and serve warm. You can keep any leftover baba ghanoush, covered, in the refrigerator for 3–5 days.

Roasted eggplant dip

Judit Gulyás, Debrecen, Hungary

Gluten-free • Serves 4–6

1 eggplant (aubergine)
1 kapia pepper or small red capsicum (bell pepper)
1 small onion, sliced
Himalayan salt or sea salt and freshly ground black pepper
1 tablespoon extra virgin olive oil

Preheat the oven to 180°C (350°C/gas 4).

Put the eggplant and pepper or capsicum into an oven bag and roast until they are soft, about 40–50 minutes. The pepper or capsicum should be brownish and the eggplant almost black. (Or roast them on the barbecue to add a smoky flavour.) Leave them to cool, peel and cut into smaller slices or dices.

Cook the onion in a heavy-based frying pan over medium heat until translucent. Make sure to add a bit of water if the onion begins to stick too much and take on colour. If some pieces get brownish, they can add extra taste to the dip. Add the eggplant and pepper or capsicum and cook for about 5 minutes. Spice the food with salt and pepper.

Put all the ingredients in a blender or food processor and process until smooth.

TIP: Serve this dip at a barbecue party with toast, homemade grissini and raw vegetables.

Bean dip

Penelope Thomas, Sheffield, United Kingdom

Serves 4

heaped ⅓ cup sun-dried tomatoes (the dry kind, not in a jar of oil)
1 large handful of flat-leaf (Italian) parsley
2 × 400 g (14 oz) cans cannellini beans or butter beans (or 1 can of each is nice, too),
  rinsed and drained
½ garlic clove, or a whole clove if small (or if you really like garlic), peeled
a tiny bit of American mustard, maybe ¼ teaspoon
water, as needed

Pour boiling water onto the sun-dried tomatoes and soak for at least 20 minutes, to soften and wash off the excess salt. Rinse and put into a food processor.

Add the parsley, beans, garlic and mustard. Blend the mixture until creamy and smooth, or to your preferred consistency (this can take a while!). It is often necessary to add a splash or two of water, especially when using cannellini beans—less is needed with a mixture of beans, or with butter beans.

TIP: This dip is lovely on warm or toasted spelt bread with flaxseed oil, and also in jacket potatoes. Both options are also very filling as a main meal with a salad.

Spicy sweet potato hummus

Ingrid Adelsberger, Los Angeles, United States

Makes 3–4 cups

2 sweet potatoes, unpeeled
1–2 tablespoons extra virgin olive oil
2 cups cooked chickpeas (garbanzo beans) or 1 × 400 g (14 oz) can chickpeas,
   rinsed and drained
2 tablespoons tahini
2–3 garlic cloves, peeled
zest of ½ lemon
juice of 1 lemon
sea salt
¼ teaspoon ground cumin
1½ teaspoons cayenne pepper or ½ teaspoon smoked paprika
sourdough or wholegrain bread or crudités, to serve

Preheat the oven to 200°C (400°F/gas 6).

Bake the sweet potatoes on the middle rack in the oven or in a baking dish for 45–60 minutes. When they're cooked, they should yield to a gentle squeeze. Set aside to cool. Once the sweet potatoes have cooled, use a knife to peel them, then roughly chop.

Toss the sweet potato, 1 tablespoon of oil, the chickpeas, tahini, garlic, lemon zest and juice, salt and cumin in a food processor. Blend well and add more oil if the hummus is too thick. Garnish with the cayenne pepper or smoked paprika and serve with bread or crudités.

TIP: To speed up the process, you can microwave the sweet potato. Use a fork to prick the sweet potatoes all over, then microwave them on high for 8–10 minutes, turning them once.

Soy quark (cottage cheese)

Jo, Freshwater, Australia

Serves 4

4 cups soy milk
juice of ½ lemon, plus extra if needed

Heat the soy milk to 70–80°C (150–175°F). Don't boil it, or it will curdle. Add the lemon juice and stir. It should curdle, but if it doesn't, add more lemon juice but note that this will give it a more lemony flavour.

Place in a colander lined with muslin (cheesecloth), strain overnight in the fridge and weight it if you prefer your quark to be firmer.

TIP: This makes a yummy quark substitute and has a light lemony flavour. It is good on crackers or in sandwiches and salads.

Spinach dip

Ingrid Adelsberger, Los Angeles, United States

Serves 4–6

400 g (14 oz) silken tofu
⅓ cup cashew nuts, soaked in water
  overnight, drained
⅓ cup nutritional yeast
2 tablespoons apple cider vinegar
½ teaspoon sea salt
175 g (6 oz) English spinach leaves

1 onion, finely chopped
2 garlic cloves, finely chopped
100 g (3½ oz) water chestnuts, diced
smoked paprika, to garnish
crackers, sourdough or wholegrain
  bread or crudités, to serve

Combine the tofu, cashews, nutritional yeast, vinegar and salt in a high-speed blender and blend until a smooth purée forms. You may have to scrape down the side and whiz again to achieve a completely smooth consistency. Set aside.

Place the spinach in a large saucepan of boiling water and boil until the spinach is wilted, 1–2 minutes. Drain, rinse with cold water and squeeze out the excess water. Finely chop the spinach and set aside.

Cook the onion in a heavy-based frying pan over medium heat until translucent. Make sure to add 1–2 tablespoons of water if the onion begins to stick too much and take on colour. You are just looking to soften the onion at this stage and remove its raw flavour. Add the garlic and cook, stirring, for 2–3 minutes.

Stir in the water chestnuts and spinach and sauté to heat through. Turn down the heat to low, add the tofu and cashew purée and stir constantly until heated through. Adjust salt to taste.

Put into a serving bowl and sprinkle on the smoked paprika. Serve with crackers, bread or crudités.

 NOTE: Do not omit the smoked paprika; it gives the dish an extra kick.

Carrot dip

Hester Dekker, Vught, The Netherlands

Serves 4

400 g (14 oz) carrots, thickly sliced
2 tablespoons extra virgin olive oil, plus extra for drizzling
1 teaspoon ground cumin
½ teaspoon ground cinnamon
1 teaspoon sweet paprika
2–3 cm (¾–1¼ inch) piece of ginger, grated
2 garlic cloves, crushed
1 teaspoon honey
juice of 1 lemon
sea salt and freshly ground black pepper
1 tablespoon pine nuts, lightly toasted (optional)

Preheat the oven to 200°C (400°F/gas 6).

Toss the carrot with the olive oil in a baking dish. Roast for 30–40 minutes until tender. Remove from the oven and crush with a fork. Stir in the cumin, cinnamon, paprika, ginger, garlic, honey and lemon juice and season to taste. Alternatively, you can blitz the roasted carrot in a food processor with the rest of the ingredients.

Spoon the dip into a serving bowl, drizzle with some extra olive oil and sprinkle over the pine nuts (if using) and serve.

Onion bhajis

Susan Doumbos, Mornington, Australia

Makes 10 bhajis

3 onions, sliced

3–4 garlic cloves, chopped

½ teaspoon sea salt

½ teaspoon ground turmeric

½ teaspoon chilli powder

1 teaspoon ground coriander

1 teaspoon ground cumin

½ teaspoon ground ginger

85 g (3 oz) chickpea flour (besan)
  or brown rice flour

2½ tablespoons tomato passata

drizzle of extra virgin olive oil

Preheat the oven to 180°C (350°C/gas 4).

Cook the onion in a heavy-based frying pan over medium heat until translucent. Make sure to add a bit of water if the onion begins to stick too much and take on colour. You are just looking to soften the onion at this stage and remove its raw flavour.

Add the garlic, salt and all spices to the pan, stir well and then turn off the heat. Add the flour, mix well and stir in the passata. (Verge on less rather than more, otherwise the mixture will be too runny.)

Spoon onto a baking tray lined with baking paper (make the bhajis whatever size you like, but note they will take a bit longer to cook if you make them bigger) and bake for 10 minutes.

Remove from the oven and drizzle with a tiny bit of oil (I use 1 teaspoon per 3–4 bhajis). Return to the oven for another 10 minutes, or until brown.

TIPS: These freeze really well. I just put them on a chopping board lined with baking paper and freeze for a few hours before putting them in a snap-lock bag. Then I simply take them out and warm them for 20 minutes at 180°C (350°C/gas 4). You can enjoy them with a curry for dinner and also with a salad for lunch.

Angel's eggs

Nienke Sanders, The Hague, The Netherlands

Serves 8

400 g (14 oz) can chickpeas (garbanzo beans), rinsed and drained

juice of ½ lemon

4 tablespoons water

3 tablespoons extra virgin olive oil

2 tablespoons tahini

½ teaspoon ground cumin

½ teaspoon ground paprika

½ teaspoon ground turmeric

½ teaspoon ground coriander

sea salt and freshly ground black pepper

8 hard-boiled eggs, halved lengthways and yolks removed

smoked paprika, to garnish

finely chopped coriander (cilantro), to garnish

Put the chickpeas, lemon juice, water, olive oil, tahini, cumin, paprika, turmeric, ground coriander and salt and pepper in a food processor or blender and blend until smooth.

Spoon the chickpea mixture into a piping (icing) bag and fill the cavity in each halved egg. Garnish each stuffed egg with some smoked paprika and chopped coriander.

TIP: These are perfect party food and can also be served as a side dish or entrée.

Vietnamese summer rolls

Dat Nguyen, New York, United States

Makes 8

115 g (4 oz) wholegrain vermicelli

8 large rice paper wrappers

2 carrots, thinly sliced with a vegetable peeler

½ cucumber, cut into julienne

½ cup bean sprouts

½ cup chopped coriander (cilantro)

½ cup chopped mint

½ cup chopped basil

450 g (1 lb) cooked prawns (shrimp), peeled and deveined, cut into small pieces

For the sauce

½ cup OMS-safe hoisin sauce

2 tablespoons almond butter

1 tablespoon sriracha (or other hot chilli sauce)

Place the noodles in a bowl and cover with boiling water. Allow them to sit for 3 minutes, or until softened. Drain and rinse under cool water. Set aside.

Prepare all your ingredients. Fill a large shallow container with warm water and dip one rice paper wrapper in it for about 5 seconds. If it's not soft after 5 seconds, any residual water will make it easy to roll up.

Place the rice paper wrapper on a plate and, on the bottom half, start layering the noodles, then the carrot, cucumber, sprouts, herbs and finally the prawns. Fold the sides of the wrapper over the filling and roll it up like a burrito. Repeat for the remaining rice paper wrappers and filling ingredients.

Mix all the sauce ingredients together in a small bowl.

Serve the summer rolls with the dipping sauce.

Spicy marinated zucchini

Ingrid Adelsberger, Los Angeles, United States

Serves 4–6

4 zucchini (courgettes), thinly sliced

2–3 spring onions (scallions), thinly sliced

1 tablespoon extra virgin olive oil

2 tablespoons rice vinegar

1 teaspoon sesame oil

1 teaspoon dried red chilli flakes

1–2 garlic cloves, finely chopped

1 teaspoon sea salt

½ teaspoon freshly ground black pepper

Toss the zucchini and onion with the olive oil, vinegar, sesame oil, chilli flakes and garlic and season with salt and pepper. Refrigerate for at least 1 hour before serving, so the zucchini can absorb the flavours.

 TIP: This can be used as an appetiser or a side dish.

Sicilian fennel salad

Hester Dekker, Vught, The Netherlands

Serves 4

2 tablespoons raisins

2 fennel bulbs, thinly sliced

2½ tablespoons flaxseed oil or extra virgin olive oil or a blend of the two

2½ tablespoons white wine vinegar

sea salt and freshly ground black pepper

2 oranges, peeled and thinly sliced

2 heaped cups rocket (arugula) leaves

100 g (3½ oz) almonds, toasted and roughly chopped

2 tablespoons pistachio nuts, toasted and roughly chopped

Preheat the oven to 220°C (425°F/gas 7). Line a baking tray with baking paper.

Soak the raisins in a bowl of water while you prepare the other ingredients. Place the fennel on the prepared tray and roast for 10 minutes.

Whisk the oil and vinegar in a bowl to make a vinaigrette. Add salt and pepper to taste.

Drain the raisins. Spread the fennel, orange slices and rocket on a serving dish. Sprinkle with the vinaigrette and cover with the nuts and raisins.

Green papaya salad

Jo, Freshwater, Australia

Serves 2

3 garlic cloves, peeled

pinch of sea salt

2 tablespoons tiny dried shrimp, rinsed and drained (from Asian shops)

8–10 cherry tomatoes, quartered

2 snake beans or 4 green beans, cut into 1 cm (½ inch) lengths

4 bird's eye chillies, or to taste

2 cups shredded green papaya (green mango is also very good!
  I often use a mixture)

Dressing

3–4 tablespoons shaved palm sugar

2–3 tablespoons fish sauce

2–3 tablespoons lime juice

1 tablespoon tamarind paste

For this recipe you will need a large mortar and pestle, which can be purchased at most Asian stores.

Pound the garlic and salt together using your mortar and pestle. Add the dried shrimp and pound to a paste. Then add the cherry tomatoes and beans and pound less vigorously and add the chillies. Add the green papaya, bruise it with the pestle and mix it all together.

Mix the palm sugar, fish sauce, lime juice and tamarind paste to make a sweet, sour, salty dressing. Taste and adjust the balance, if needed, before you add it to the salad.

Mix the dressing with the salad.

TIP: Serve with rice and raw vegetables—such as cabbage, beans and betel leaves—and wedges of lime.

Tuna with avocado salad

Hester Dekker, Vught, The Netherlands

Serves 4

1 red onion, finely chopped
360 g (12¾ oz) red and yellow cherry tomatoes, quartered
2 avocados, finely chopped
4 fresh or frozen tuna steaks
1 loaf of good-tasting bread
2 heaped cups rocket (arugula) leaves

Dressing
zest and juice of 1 lime
2 tablespoons flaxseed oil
1 bunch of coriander (cilantro), finely chopped
freshly ground black pepper

Place the onion, tomato and avocado in a bowl.

To make the dressing, in a small bowl mix the lime zest and juice with the oil. Add the coriander and season with pepper (and salt if you like) to taste.

Heat the barbecue or preheat the oven to 180°C (350°F/gas 4).

Season the tuna with pepper then place it on the barbecue or in the oven for 5–10 minutes, turning the tuna halfway. The cooking time depends on the thickness of the tuna and how you like it cooked.

In the meantime, cut the bread into eight slices and toast them.

For each person, place two slices of bread on a plate, put the rocket leaves on top. Cut the tuna into slices and place on top of the rocket. Cover with the avocado salad and add the dressing, if you like.

Carrot walnut salad

Jessica van Esch, County Kerry, Ireland
Serves 4

8 carrots, shredded (a food processor with a shredder attachment
  works well for this)
2 tart apples (such as paula red or granny smith), peeled and shredded
  in a food processor

Dressing
1½ tablespoons olive oil or flaxseed oil
3 tablespoons apple cider vinegar
¾ cup chopped walnuts
½ cup raisins
1 tablespoon honey
½ teaspoon sea salt
½ teaspoon freshly ground black pepper

Combine the carrot and apple in a large bowl. Whisk together the dressing ingredients in a bowl and toss through the carrot and apple.

This salad can be eaten right away, though letting the flavours mingle for an hour or two is nice. Serve chilled or at room temperature.

Beetroot and walnut salad

Paul Tudor-Ward, Llandysul, Wales

Serves 4

680 g (1 lb 8 oz) beetroot (beets), peeled and diced
extra virgin olive oil cooking spray
1 handful of walnuts
10 anchovy fillets, drained
4 large handfuls of rocket (arugula) leaves, roughly torn
1 garlic clove, finely chopped

Dressing
3 tablespoons balsamic vinegar
3 tablespoons walnut oil

Preheat the oven to 180°C (350°F/gas 4).

Spread the beetroot on a baking tray and spray with the extra virgin olive oil. Roast until cooked through and slightly crispy.

Combine the dressing ingredients in a bowl and whisk.

Mix all the ingredients in a bowl and toss with the dressing.

 TIP: For a more robust dish, toss pasta shapes into the salad.

Tuna and cannellini bean salad

Abba Renshaw, Auckland, New Zealand

Serves 2

2 × 185 g (6½ oz) cans tuna in water, drained
400 g (14 oz) can cannellini beans, rinsed and drained
½ red onion, finely chopped
flat-leaf (Italian) parsley, chopped
juice of 1 lemon
a good glug of extra virgin olive oil
sea salt and freshly ground black pepper
crusty bread, to serve

Mix all the ingredients together and season. Serve cold with crusty bread.

Warm rice salad
Ingrid Adelsberger, Los Angeles, United States
Gluten-free • Serves 4

1 cup long-grain brown rice, cooked
12 pitted kalamata olives, chopped
1 cup chopped cherry tomatoes
3–4 radishes, shredded
½ fennel bulb, shredded
¼ cup chopped parsley or basil

Mix the rice with the remaining ingredients and serve with the Mustard Vinaigrette (see recipe, page 232). Alternatively, you could use the Gawler Foundation Salad Dressing (see recipe, page 229).

TIP: This dish was first made for me by a chef friend so I had something OMS-friendly to eat at an event. It's a great side dish with salmon and steamed greens or beans.

Chickpea salad with mint
Ingrid Adelsberger, Los Angeles, United States
Serves 2

425 g (15 oz) can chickpeas (garbanzo beans), drained and rinsed

½ cup diced cherry tomatoes

½ cup diced cucumber

½ cup diced red onion

3 tablespoons finely chopped flat-leaf (Italian) parsley

3 tablespoons finely chopped mint

6 black olives, diced

sea salt and freshly ground black pepper

1 tablespoon extra virgin olive oil or flaxseed oil

1 tablespoon red wine vinegar

Combine the chickpeas, tomato, cucumber, onion, herbs and olives in a bowl and season with salt and pepper. Mix in the oil and vinegar and enjoy.

TIP: This is so simple and delicious. It's a great starter or salad in summer and keeps well in the fridge for up to 2 days.

Tuna salad

Ingrid Adelsberger, Los Angeles, United States
Serves 2

200 g (7 oz) can tuna, drained and flaked
⅓ cup Silken Tofu Mayonnaise (see recipe, page 220)
1 tablespoon nutritional yeast
⅛ teaspoon dried onion flakes
¼ teaspoon curry powder
1 tablespoon dried parsley
1 teaspoon dried dill
pinch of garlic powder
3 tablespoons sweet pickle relish or sweet pickles
1 celery stalk, finely chopped
crackers or bread, to serve

In a bowl, stir together the tuna, mayonnaise, nutritional yeast and dried onion flakes. Season with the curry powder, parsley, dill and garlic powder and add the relish or sweet pickles (if using) and celery. Mix well and serve with the crackers or on bread for lunch.

Nutritional yeast is really nice for replacing cheese in any dish. I use it because it reminds me of parmesan.
Juraj Brozovi´c, Zagreb, Croatia

Mexican black bean salad

Rebecca Hoover, Saint Paul, United States

Serves 4

3 cups canned black beans, drained and rinsed

1½ cups frozen corn kernels, cooked and rinsed with cold water until chilled

1 cup diced tomato

½ cup chopped spring onions (scallions)

½ cup roughly chopped coriander (cilantro)

1–2 tablespoons very finely chopped jalapeno chilli

90 ml (3 fl oz) lime juice

1 tablespoon flaxseed oil (optional)

sea salt

corn tortillas, to serve (optional)

Place all the ingredients except the tortillas in a large bowl and toss to combine. Jalapeno chillies vary greatly in heat, so it is smart to start with 1 tablespoon and adjust as needed. Serve with warmed and lightly salted corn tortillas, if desired. Enjoy!

TIP: A salad that combines beans with corn provides complete protein and is a great dish to bring to a buffet. It ensures we will have something filling to eat when we are among meat eaters.

Whole-wheat grain salad

Ingrid Adelsberger, Los Angeles, United States

Serves 2

½ cup whole-wheat grain (wheat berries), rinsed and drained

1 cup roughly chopped kale

1 celery stalk, finely chopped

½ cup cherry tomatoes

1–2 tablespoons dried cranberries

½ spring onion (scallion), chopped

½ cup cannellini beans

sea salt and freshly ground black pepper

4–6 crushed walnuts, to crumble on top

extra virgin olive oil or flaxseed oil and balsamic vinegar, to drizzle on top

Place the wheat grain in a small saucepan and cook in salted water for about 1 hour until al dente. Drain well.

In the meantime, steam the kale until it's bright green, about 5 minutes.

In a large bowl, combine all the ingredients except the walnuts and oil and vinegar. Crumble the walnuts on top and sprinkle over the oil and vinegar.

TIP: This crunchy and delicious salad—I love the texture of it—keeps well in the fridge for 1–2 days.

Quinoa detox salad

Natalie Harvey, London, United Kingdom

Gluten-free • Serves 4

1 cup quinoa, thoroughly rinsed

2 cups vegetable stock (homemade—for a recipe, see page 110)

3 small sweet potatoes

1 × 400 g (14 oz) can corn kernels, drained and rinsed

1 × 400 g (14 oz) can black beans, drained and rinsed

1 cup chopped red capsicum (bell pepper)

1 cup halved cherry tomatoes

3 tablespoons finely chopped coriander (cilantro)

sea salt and freshly ground black pepper

3 tablespoons lime juice

balsamic vinegar, to drizzle (optional)

Combine the quinoa and vegetable stock in a saucepan and bring to the boil. Reduce the heat to low, cover and simmer until the quinoa is tender and most of the liquid has been absorbed, 15–20 minutes. Fluff with a fork.

Meanwhile, pierce the sweet potatoes with a fork and cook them in the microwave for 5–6 minutes, or until tender. Remove and cool before peeling and chopping into smaller pieces.

In a large bowl, combine the corn, black beans, capsicum and cherry tomatoes. Add the quinoa and sweet potato and mix together. Add the coriander and season to taste with salt and pepper and the lime juice. Drizzle with the vinegar, if desired.

Store leftovers in the fridge in an airtight container.

Quinoa and pomegranate salad

Nienke Sanders, The Hague, Netherlands

Serves 6

150 g (5½ oz) quinoa, rinsed
vegetable stock (homemade—for a recipe, see page 110)
½ cup pine nuts
pinch of sea salt
seeds of 1 pomegranate
½ bunch of coriander (cilantro), chopped
½ bunch of flat-leaf (Italian) parsley, chopped
juice of 1 lime
2 teaspoons tamari or soy sauce
4 tablespoons extra virgin olive oil

Cook the quinoa in the vegetable stock according to the instructions on the packet. (Alternatively, cook the quinoa in water with 1 teaspoon of herbal salt added.) Set aside to cool.

Combine the pine nuts and salt in a frying pan and toast until light brown. Set aside to cool.

Fluff the cooled quinoa with a fork and mix with the pine nuts, pomegranate seeds, herbs, lime juice, tamari or soy sauce and olive oil in a bowl.

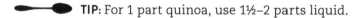 **TIP:** For 1 part quinoa, use 1½–2 parts liquid.

German-inspired potato salad

Pam Schartner, Tranmere, Australia

Serves 4

6 large potatoes, scrubbed and eyes removed
2 handfuls of green beans, topped and tailed and cut into shorter lengths
1 handful of frozen peas or pea and sweet corn mix
6 dill gherkins (pickles), cut into thin rounds
1 tablespoon dill gherkin (pickle) juice
1 bunch of dill, chopped
about 4 tablespoons Gawler Foundation Salad Dressing (see recipe, page 229)
freshly ground black pepper

Gently steam the potatoes until tender; test with a skewer. When they are cool enough to handle, peel them, if preferred, and slice.

Steam the beans for a few minutes, ensuring they are still crunchy. Set aside to cool.

Steam the peas/sweet corn for a few minutes. Set aside to cool.

Combine the potato, gherkins and gherkin juice in a bowl, gently mix in the beans and peas/sweet corn and add most of the dill and 2 tablespoons of dressing. Set aside for at least an hour to allow the flavours to develop. Mix again and taste. You may need to add the remaining dressing (this depends on the potatoes used). Garnish with the remaining dill and season with pepper.

NOTE: Traditionally, chopped boiled eggs are added to the salad at the final stage, but this is not OMS-friendly. If you like, replace with chopped hard-boiled egg whites.

Green salad with pine nuts

Wendy Wood, Murchison, New Zealand

Serves 4–6

150 g (5½ oz) mixed lettuce leaves

2 avocados, sliced or cut into chunks

1 cucumber, cut into fingers or batons

1 tablespoon Gawler Foundation Salad Dressing (page 229) or Simple Honey Lemon
  Dressing (page 227), or to taste

½ cup pine nuts, lightly toasted

Toss the lettuce, avocado and cucumber in the dressing of your choice and top
with the pine nuts. Lovely served on a big platter. The contrast between the
crunch of the cucumber and pine nuts with the creamy avocado is delicious.

Zucchini and burghul (bulgur) salad

Wendy Wood, Murchison, New Zealand

Serves 4–6

1 cup burghul (bulgur)
2 cups water
zest of 1 lemon
juice of 2 lemons
3 tablespoons flaxseed oil
4–5 zucchini (courgettes), sliced into thin rounds
1 red onion, sliced
1 handful of mixed mint, basil and flat-leaf (Italian) parsley leaves,
  roughly chopped
sea salt and freshly ground black pepper

Combine the burghul, water, lemon zest and juice of 1 lemon in a saucepan over medium–low heat, cover and cook for 10–15 minutes. Fluff with a fork, tip into a bowl and stir in the flaxseed oil and the remaining lemon juice.

Grill (broil) the zucchini and red onion until they are softened and lightly browned. I use a chargrill pan.

Toss the zucchini, red onion and herbs into the burghul mixture and season well with salt and pepper.

Tomato salad with ginger and mint

Ingrid Adelsberger, Los Angeles, United States

Gluten-free • Serves 4

450 g (1 lb) yellow and red cherry tomatoes, quartered
1 teaspoon extra virgin olive oil
1 teaspoon finely grated ginger
sea salt and freshly ground black pepper
1 handful of mint leaves, torn or roughly chopped
1 teaspoon finely grated lemon zest
1 tablespoon lemon juice

Toss the tomatoes with the oil and ginger and season with salt and pepper. Just before serving, toss with the mint and lemon zest and juice.

 Introduce your family and friends to the OMS website so they can no longer say, 'I have no idea what you eat and don't eat.' Don't let anyone think you are a 'fussy eater'. You're not—you are looking after yourself in the best way possible.

Jill Pack, London, United Kingdom

Salad in a jar

Leanne Shearer, Berwick, Australia

Serves 1

When I know I'm going out where there will not be much food choice, I take my own meal. A great and easy option is a layered meal in a jar. It keeps well in the refrigerator for a few days, so you can make it well ahead of time, and is extremely easy to transport, as you use a jar with a screw-top lid. The quantities depend on the size of the jar and your personal taste.

Layer the salad ingredients as follows:

1. Bottom layer: pasta, burghul (bulgur), couscous or quinoa
2. Next layer: salad dressing of your choice or soy yoghurt
3. Next layer: fish of choice—salmon, tuna, sardines, etc.
4. Next layer: salad ingredients—cucumber, tomatoes, olives, grated carrot, chickpeas, lentils, etc.
5. Follow with a layer of soft salad ingredients: lettuce, baby spinach leaves, rocket (arugula), alfalfa, etc.
6. Then the final layer: herbs, seeds and nuts of choice.

To serve, simply invert onto a serving dish and enjoy.

SOUPS

Miso soup

Ingrid Adelsberger, Los Angeles, United States
Gluten-free • Serves 2

2 tablespoons red or white miso paste
115 g (4 oz) silken or firm tofu, cut into 1 cm (½ inch) cubes
1–2 spring onions (scallions), thinly sliced

Dashi
2 cups water
5 cm (2 inch) piece of kombu (dried black kelp)
½ cup loosely packed bonito flakes (katsuobushi)

To make the dashi, combine the water and kombu in a saucepan over medium heat. Remove the kombu just as the water comes to the boil. Add the bonito flakes and allow the water come to a rapid simmer. Simmer for about 1 minute, then remove the pan from the heat and leave the bonito flakes to steep for 5 minutes. Strain the dashi and add more water if necessary to make 2 cups.

Pour the dashi into a saucepan and bring to a simmer over medium–high heat. Place the miso in a cup, and pour about ½ cup of dashi over the miso. Whisk to dissolve the miso.

Pour the dissolved miso into the simmering dashi, reduce the heat to medium–low and add the tofu. Simmer for 1–2 minutes, just long enough to warm the tofu. Do not allow the miso to boil once the tofu has been added. Scatter the spring onion over the top. Pour the miso soup into individual bowls and serve.

TIPS: If you don't have kombu and bonito flakes, substitute 2 cups of vegetable stock (for a recipe, see page 110).

Miso is best served at once. It will settle a bit as it sits in the dashi; before eating, whisk briefly with a spoon.

Ramen

Dat Nguyen and Ingrid Adelsberger, Los Angeles, United States

Serves 4

1 onion, roughly chopped

5 garlic cloves, roughly chopped

7.5 cm (3 inch) piece of ginger, peeled and diced

6 cups vegetable stock (homemade—for a recipe, see page 110)

1 tablespoon tamari or soy sauce, plus more to taste

15 g (½ oz) dried shiitake mushrooms

1 tablespoon white or yellow miso paste (make sure it's OMS-friendly)

225 g (8 oz) ramen noodles (make sure they're OMS-friendly)

1 teaspoon sesame oil (optional)

Suggested toppings

½ cup finely chopped spring onions (scallions)

280 g (10 oz) extra firm tofu, chopped

½ cup corn kernels

wakame and nori

enoki or other mushrooms

3 tablespoons quartered cherry tomatoes

3 tablespoons chopped cucumber

4 egg whites, boiled

shichimi (Japanese chilli) or chilli flakes

Place the onion in a large, heavy-based saucepan over medium heat and cook, stirring occasionally, for 5–8 minutes until translucent. Add a bit of water if the onion begins to stick too much and take on colour. Then add the garlic and ginger and cook for 3–5 minutes until fragrant. (Add more water if needed.)

Add 1 cup of vegetable stock to deglaze the pan and, with a whisk or wooden spoon, scrape up any bits that have stuck to the bottom (this enhances the flavour). Add the remaining vegetable stock, the tamari or soy sauce and shiitake mushrooms and stir. Bring to a simmer, then reduce the heat to low and cover. Simmer, stirring occasionally, for at least 1 hour, up to 2–3 hours. The longer the broth cooks, the better the flavour be. Taste the broth and adjust the seasoning to taste, adding more tamari or soy sauce, if desired. Stir in the miso paste and let it simmer for 1 hour. Adjust if necessary.

Fill a large saucepan with water and bring to the boil. Add the ramen noodles and cook according to the packet instructions. Drain and set aside.

Strain the broth, reserving the mushrooms for serving. (Save the onion, garlic and ginger for serving as well, if you like, or discard them.) To serve, divide the ramen noodles between four serving bowls and top with the broth, the mushrooms, the desired toppings and a few drops of sesame oil (if using).

NOTE: This recipe is inspired by a restaurant in New York that has the best vegan ramen with about ten different toppings. The broth can be kept in an airtight container in the fridge for up to 5 days and up to 1 month in the freezer.

Cauliflower soup

Kathryn Hughes, Wiltshire, United Kingdom

Serves 2

a few cauliflower florets

3–4 thin red chilli slices

liberal sprinkling of golden flaxseeds

½ vegetable stock cube (make sure it's OMS-friendly)

½ carrot

1 teaspoon ground turmeric

600 ml (21 fl oz) water (I use distilled water)

½ onion, peeled

Boil all the ingredients together, blend and add more water if necessary.

Chilled cucumber soup

Jack McNulty, Zurich, Switzerland

Serves 2

about 120 g (4¼ oz) white bread, crusts removed

1 garlic clove, peeled

1 teaspoon sea salt

several dashes of Tabasco sauce

3 tablespoons sherry vinegar

3 tablespoons olive oil

1 handful of peppermint leaves

3 tablespoons chopped flat-leaf (Italian) parsley, plus extra to serve

3 tablespoons chopped coriander (cilantro), plus extra to serve

2 cucumbers, peeled and deseeded

150 ml (5 fl oz) iced water

1 large green capsicum (bell pepper), finely chopped

freshly ground black pepper

soy yoghurt, to serve

In a large bowl, pour cold water over the bread to cover and let it soak for 5 minutes. Drain the bread in a strainer and lightly press out the excess water. Put the bread in a blender and add the garlic, salt, Tabasco sauce, vinegar, oil and herbs.

Roughly chop one of the cucumbers and add it to the blender. Purée on high speed until the mixture is very smooth and uniformly green (you can use a food processor, but the texture will not be as smooth). Blend in the iced water. Pour the soup into a bowl or plastic container.

Finely chop the remaining cucumber and stir into the soup with the capsicum. Season well and refrigerate, covered, for several hours. Serve in small bowls and garnish with a touch of soy yoghurt and the extra chopped herbs.

Nutrient broth

Carl Herring, Setagaya-ku, Hanegi, Japan

Serves 2

185 g (6½ oz) udon noodles

2 handfuls of mushrooms (such as shiitake, oyster, chestnut), torn

1 carrot, sliced

1 onion, sliced

2 bok choy (pak choy), roughly chopped

1 bunch of flat-leaf (Italian) parsley or coriander (cilantro), roughly torn or chopped

100 ml (3½ fl oz) cooking sake

3–4 tablespoons kombu tsuyu (Japanese fish and seaweed stock)

1 tablespoon tamari or soy sauce

ground turmeric, freshly ground black pepper and flaxseed oil, to serve (optional)

Bring a large saucepan of water to the boil and add the udon noodles. When the noodles have relaxed into the pan, add the vegetables, herbs, sake, kombu tsuyu and tamari or soy sauce and bring to the boil again. Reduce the heat and simmer until the noodles are done, about 10 minutes.

Serve with the turmeric, black pepper and flaxseed oil to taste, if desired.

Cream of broccoli soup

Ingrid Adelsberger, Los Angeles, United States

Gluten-free • Serves 3–4

1 onion, chopped
1 potato, peeled and chopped
6 cups vegetable stock (homemade—for a recipe, see page 110)
4 cups chopped broccoli florets and stems
½ cup almond milk (or other preferred plant-based milk)
sea salt and freshly ground black pepper
3–4 teaspoons sherry vinegar
a few spoonfuls of soy yoghurt
flat-leaf (Italian) parsley, to garnish

Heat a large, heavy-based saucepan over medium heat. Add the onion and cook, stirring occasionally, for about 10 minutes until it turns translucent. Make sure to add a bit of water if the onion begins to stick too much and take on colour. You do not want the onion to brown, you are just looking to soften it at this stage and remove its raw flavour.

Add the potato and vegetable stock and bring to the boil. Stir in the broccoli and simmer until the potato and broccoli are tender. Transfer to a blender or food processor and purée.

Return the soup to the pan and add the almond milk. Season to taste and serve warm with a splash of vinegar, a spoonful of soy yoghurt and a sprinkle of parsley.

NOTE: If you think you'll have leftovers, don't add the vinegar as the acid changes the colour of the soup.

Fish soup

Anthony, Adelaide, Australia
Serves 4

1 onion, finely chopped
1 garlic clove, finely chopped
1 large bunch of flat-leaf (Italian) parsley, roughly chopped, plus extra to serve
1 anchovy fillet (optional)
400 g (14 oz) can diced tomatoes
1 whole whiting or snook, cleaned and gutted, roughly chopped
sea salt and freshly ground black pepper
500 g (1 lb 2 oz) small pasta (optional)
3–4 fillets white fish (such as whiting, deep sea perch, flathead), roughly chopped
crusty bread, to serve

Cook the onion first in 1 tablespoon of water until translucent, then add the garlic and parsley, stirring occasionally, in a large, heavy-based saucepan over medium–low heat for a few minutes. Sometimes I add an anchovy fillet at this point to introduce the seafood flavour.

Add the diced tomatoes and reduce the heat to low. Keep stirring the tomatoes until they 'dissolve' to a thick liquid, about 10 minutes. Add the whole chopped fish and fill the pan three-quarters full with water. Season with salt and pepper (and any other spice you feel will add flavour), increase the heat and bring to the boil. Reduce the heat to low and simmer for at least 30 minutes and up to 1 hour.

Towards the end of the cooking time for the soup, if adding the pasta, bring another saucepan of water to the boil and cook the pasta according to the packet directions. Drain and return the pasta to the pan.

Using a fine sieve, strain the fish broth into the pan containing the pasta. Return to the heat, add the fish fillet pieces and cook for 3–5 minutes until the fish is just cooked through. Spoon the soup into individual bowls, garnish with the extra chopped parsley and serve with crusty bread.

Tom yum goong

Andie Austin, Dromana, Australia

Serves 4

500 g (1 lb 2 oz) raw prawns (shrimp)

4 cups water

2 tablespoons curry paste

2 tablespoons tamarind concentrate

2 teaspoons ground turmeric or grated fresh turmeric

1 bird's eye chilli, deseeded and thinly sliced (if you prefer more heat, retain the seeds)

4–8 kaffir lime leaves, central stem removed, leaf rolled and very thinly sliced

3 tablespoons fish sauce

2 tablespoons lime juice

2 teaspoons soft brown sugar

coriander (cilantro), to garnish

Peel and devein the prawns. Set the prawns aside and place the shells and heads in a large saucepan with the water. Cook over low heat, stirring regularly, for about 20 minutes. Set a strainer over a bowl large enough to hold the liquid from the pan. Strain the stock into the bowl. Throw the shells and heads away.

Return the stock to the pan, add the curry paste, tamarind, turmeric, chilli and kaffir lime leaves and cook over medium heat for 2 minutes. Add the prawns and cook for 2–3 minutes until cooked through. Remove from the heat. Add the fish sauce, lime juice and sugar, stir. Serve sprinkled with the coriander.

Haricot bean and watercress soup

Paul Tudor-Ward, Llandysul, Wales

Serves 4

1 large onion, chopped
225 g (8 oz) dried haricot beans, soaked in water overnight
6 cups vegetable stock (homemade—for a recipe, see page 110)
450 g (1 lb) potatoes, cubed
1 large bunch of watercress, land cress or rocket (arugula), roughly chopped
sea salt and freshly ground black pepper
extra virgin olive oil, to serve

Heat a large, heavy-based saucepan over medium heat. Add the onion and cook, stirring occasionally, for about 10 minutes until it turns translucent. Make sure to add a bit of water if the onion begins to stick too much and take on colour. You do not want the onion to brown, you are just looking to soften it at this stage and remove its raw flavour.

Add the beans and stock and bring to the boil. Reduce the heat and simmer until the beans are almost cooked, about 45–60 minutes.

Add the potato and simmer until tender.

Add the watercress, land cress or rocket and simmer for a few minutes more. Season and serve drizzled with a little olive oil.

Seafood chowder

Rachael Nicholls, Calgary, Canada

Serves 4

1½ cups dried yellow split peas

2 cups diced new potatoes

1 cup sliced carrots or baby carrots

5 garlic cloves, finely chopped

1 onion, finely chopped

680 g (1 lb 8 oz) your choice of seafood (I use halibut and salmon), cut into chunks

1 cup frozen peas

1 cup almond milk (or other plant-based milk), plus extra for consistency

½ cup nutritional yeast, plus extra to taste

lemon juice, to taste

1 tablespoon chopped dill

1 tablespoon chopped basil

sea salt and freshly ground black pepper

1½ teaspoons smoked paprika

1 teaspoon chilli powder

cornflour (cornstarch), to thicken

Place the split peas, potato and carrot in a large saucepan and cover with lightly salted water. Cover with the lid and bring to the boil, then reduce the heat to low and simmer for 30 minutes, or until the split peas are soft.

Add the garlic, onion and seafood to the pan and simmer until the onion is soft. Stir frequently, as this will help the potato to break down and add a thick, chowder-like texture.

Stir in the peas, almond milk, nutritional yeast, lemon juice, herbs and spices and continue to simmer, stirring frequently, until the seafood is cooked. Taste and add more lemon juice, seasoning or nutritional yeast to reach the desired balance of flavours. Add the extra almond milk and cornflour as needed to reach the desired consistency.

Potato and leek soup

Judit Gulyás, Debrecen, Hungary

Serves 4

100 g (3½ oz) leeks, pale part only, thinly sliced
500 g (1 lb 2 oz) potatoes, diced
6 cups water or vegetable stock (homemade—for a recipe, see page 110)
sea salt and freshly ground black pepper
1 tablespoon extra virgin olive oil

Sauté the leek in a little water in a heavy-based saucepan over medium heat for a few minutes until soft, stirring occasionally.

Add the potato and cook for a few minutes.

Add the water or stock, season with salt and pepper and cook until the vegetables are soft.

Take out half of the soup and blend, then add it back to the pan and reheat. Stir in the extra virgin olive oil and serve.

NOTE: This is a quick, easy and economical creamy soup for busy people.

Celery soup

Jane-Marie Harrison, Beech Cottage, United Kingdom

Serves 4

450 g (1 lb) potatoes, peeled and cut into 1 cm (½ inch) thick slices
1 large onion, roughly chopped
2 bay leaves
2¼ cups vegetable stock (homemade—for a recipe, see page 110)
1 very large bunch or 2 smaller bunches of celery
4 cups rice milk
freshly ground black pepper
celery salt or sea salt
3 tablespoons extra virgin olive oil

Put the potato, onion and bay leaves in a large saucepan, pour in the stock and bring to the boil. Reduce the heat to low and simmer, with the lid on, for about 5–6 minutes.

Meanwhile, cut off the root and any brown tips on the celery. Leave the leaves in place as they add colour to the soup. Using a food processor, finely slice the celery.

Add the celery and rice milk to the pan. Add pepper and some celery salt if you have it—ordinary salt will do—to taste. Bring back to the boil, then reduce the heat to low and simmer for 20 minutes until the celery is tender.

Remove the pan from the heat and add the extra virgin olive oil. Using a hand-held blender, blend the soup until it is the consistency you like (very smooth or with some lumps). Enjoy!

Parsnip mulligatawny soup

Wendy Wood, Murchison, New Zealand

Serves 6

185 g (6½ oz) red lentils
6 cups water or vegetable stock (homemade—for a recipe, see page 110)
½ teaspoon ground turmeric
2 parsnips, peeled and chopped
5 garlic cloves, peeled
3 cm (1¼ inch) piece of ginger, peeled
100 ml (3½ fl oz) water
1 heaped teaspoon ground cumin
1 heaped teaspoon ground coriander
¼ teaspoon cayenne pepper
sea salt and freshly ground black pepper

Place the lentils, water or stock and turmeric in a large saucepan and bring to the boil. Reduce the heat to medium and cook for 30 minutes. Add the parsnip and simmer until soft.

Purée the garlic and ginger to a paste with the water. Place in a small frying pan and cook with the rest of the spices until darkened a little.

Add to the lentil mixture and cook for another 5 minutes. Purée and season well with salt and pepper.

VARIATION: This soup can also be made with potato or pumpkin (squash) instead of the parsnip.

Sweet potato and avocado soup

Ingrid Adelsberger, Los Angeles, United States

Serves 2

½ avocado, chopped

1 sweet potato, peeled and chopped

4 cups vegetable stock (homemade—for a recipe, see page 110)

½ chipotle chilli (or ½ teaspoon chipotle chilli powder if you prefer less heat)

2 garlic cloves, chopped

1 teaspoon sea salt

1 tablespoon maple syrup

juice of 1 lime

freshly ground black pepper

soy yoghurt, to serve

finely chopped coriander (cilantro), to serve

Place the avocado, sweet potato, stock, chipotle, garlic, salt and maple syrup in a large saucepan. Bring to the boil, reduce the heat and simmer for 15–20 minutes. Discard the chipotle (if using) unless you like it *very* spicy.

Transfer the soup to a food processor and blend until smooth. Add the lime juice, season and serve with a spoonful of soy yoghurt and a sprinkle of coriander.

Indian-style curried split pea soup

Jack McNulty, Zurich, Switzerland

Serves 6–8

2 onions, finely chopped

2 celery stalks, thinly sliced

2 small green chillies (moderately hot), deseeded and finely chopped

500 g (1 lb 2 oz) dried yellow split peas, rinsed

8 cups water

5 tomatoes, roughly chopped

2 tablespoons mild curry powder or garam masala

1 teaspoon ground turmeric

400 ml (14 fl oz) rice milk

4 drops of coconut extract (optional)

2 tablespoons chopped coriander (cilantro)

sea salt

sweet paprika, to serve

chopped mint, to serve

Cook the onion, celery and chilli in a large, heavy-based saucepan over medium heat, stirring occasionally, until the onion turns translucent. Make sure to add a bit of water if they begin to stick too much and take on colour.

Add the split peas and the water and bring to the boil. Reduce the heat to low, cover and simmer gently for 10 minutes.

Stir in the tomato, cover and continue to simmer for 30 minutes, or until the split peas are tender enough to purée.

Gently heat a small saucepan over low heat, add the curry powder or garam masala and turmeric and stir for 1 minute, or until fragrant. Remove from the heat and reserve.

Partially purée the soup with a hand-held blender, then stir in the rice milk and coconut extract (if using). Bring the soup to a simmer and stir in the spice mixture, working with 1 teaspoon at a time and tasting as you go until you've added the amount you like. Stir in the coriander, adjust the seasoning and garnish with the paprika and mint.

Basic vegetable stock

Jack McNulty, Zurich, Switzerland

Makes 8 cups

2 carrots, unpeeled and sliced

2 leeks, pale part only, washed and sliced

1 fennel bulb, sliced

1 large onion, sliced

mushroom stems (optional)

2 turnips, sliced (optional)

3 garlic cloves, peeled

4 sun-dried tomatoes

1 bunch of flat-leaf (Italian) parsley or stems from 2 bunches

4 thyme sprigs

2 cloves

2 bay leaves

1 tablespoon black peppercorns

1 cup white wine (optional)

Combine the vegetables, garlic, sun-dried tomato, herbs, cloves and bay leaves in a large, heavy-based saucepan and pour in enough water to just cover. Bring to the boil, then reduce the heat to a simmer. Cover the pan and simmer for 1 hour.

Add the peppercorns and wine (if using), then simmer, uncovered, for an additional 10 minutes.

Remove from the heat and allow the stock to cool for 30–60 minutes, or longer (I leave the ingredients in the stock overnight but if you live in a very hot climate, refrigerate). Strain into a clean container, cover and refrigerate.

TIPS: To intensify their flavour and sweetness, sweat the vegetables for 10–15 minutes before adding the liquid.

Roasting the vegetables in the oven first dramatically increases the flavour intensity and sweetness.

The size of the vegetables will impact on the overall flavour. Leave them large for a mild broth or cut them up very finely for a stronger-tasting broth.

Vegan split pea and sweet potato soup

Natalie Harvey, London, United Kingdom

Serves 4

2¼ cups dried green split peas
5 celery stalks, sliced
1 large onion, chopped
1 large garlic clove, finely chopped
8 cups vegetable stock (homemade—for a recipe, see page 110)
1 sweet potato, diced
sea salt and freshly ground black pepper

Wash and drain the split peas, removing any stones.

Place the split peas, celery, onion, garlic and vegetable stock in a large saucepan, cover with the lid and bring to the boil. Reduce the heat to low and simmer, cracking the lid open slightly and stirring occasionally, for 15 minutes.

Add the sweet potato and cook for 20–30 minutes until the split peas are soft and the soup looks creamy. Season with salt and pepper and enjoy!

Tomato soup

Jane-Marie Harrison, Beech Cottage, United Kingdom

Serves 6

1 large potato, sweet potato or parsnip, peeled and chopped
1 large onion, chopped
2 × 400 g (14 oz) cans chopped or whole tomatoes
whatever fresh herbs you have to hand
a good pinch of curry powder
2 tablespoons tomato paste
1–3 cups rice milk (or whatever alternative to dairy milk you have)
salt and freshly ground black pepper

Place the potato, sweet potato or parsnip in a saucepan of boiling water and cook until tender. Drain.

Cook the onion in a large, heavy-based frying pan over medium heat until translucent. Make sure to add a bit of water if the onion begins to stick too much and take on colour. You are just looking to soften the onion at this stage and remove its raw flavour.

Stir in the tomatoes; potato, sweet potato or parsnip; herbs; curry powder; and tomato paste. Bring to the boil, reduce the heat to low and simmer gently for 5 minutes.

Blitz with a hand-held blender, then add enough milk to make the soup the consistency you prefer. Taste and add salt and pepper to your liking. Reheat but do not bring to the boil.

TOFU
AND
TEMPEH
DISHES

Tempeh kebabs with barbecue sauce

Ingrid Adelsberger, Los Angeles, United States

Serves 4

Barbecue Sauce (see recipe, page 215)
450 g (1 lb) tempeh, cut into 4 cm (1½ inch) pieces
1 large red capsicum (bell pepper), cut into 4 cm (1½ inch) pieces
1 large zucchini (courgette), cut into 4 cm (1½ inch) pieces
1 large onion, cut into 4 cm (1½ inch) pieces
225 g (8 oz) button mushrooms, washed and trimmed
bamboo skewers, soaked in water for 20 minutes

Pour the barbecue sauce into a bowl and add the tempeh and vegetables. Toss to coat well and allow to marinate in the fridge for 2 hours or overnight.

Divide the vegetables and tempeh evenly and thread alternating ingredients onto the skewers.

Heat the barbecue to medium–high. Place the skewers on the barbecue and cook, basting occasionally with the sauce, for 7–10 minutes until the vegetables are tender and everything is browned. (You can also do this in a chargrill pan and cook for 8–10 minutes on medium–high heat.) Serve immediately with the remaining sauce.

Baked tofu

Gili Ginossar, Jerusalem, Israel

Serves 4–6

800 g–1 kg (1 lb 12 oz–2 lb 4 oz) fresh firm tofu, cut into fingers

Sauce
½ cup tamari or soy sauce
2 tablespoons date syrup, honey or agave syrup
2 garlic cloves, finely chopped
1 tablespoon ground ginger
1–2 tablespoons water

Mix all the sauce ingredients in a shallow bowl, add the tofu fingers and gently toss to coat evenly. Leave for 25–30 minutes.

Preheat the oven to 180°C (350°F/gas 4). Line a baking dish with baking paper.

Remove the tofu from the marinade and place in the prepared dish. Pour the marinade over the tofu. Bake for 10 minutes, turn the tofu fingers and bake for a further 10 minutes. Serve with your favourite grains and vegetables.

Tempeh chilli

Ingrid Adelsberger, Los Angeles, United States

Serves 4

1 onion, diced

3 garlic cloves, finely chopped

225 g (8 oz) tempeh, coarsely grated or finely crumbled

1 large green capsicum (bell pepper), diced

1 large celery stalk, diced

1 cup vegetable stock (homemade—for a recipe, see page 110)

1 cup water

1 cup tomato passata

425 g (15 oz) can kidney beans, drained and rinsed (or 1½ cups cooked)

425 g (15 oz) can pinto beans, drained and rinsed (or 1½ cups cooked)

1 teaspoon dried oregano

1 teaspoon ground cumin

2 teaspoons chilli powder

¼ teaspoon ground cinnamon

½–1 teaspoon sea salt

½ teaspoon chilli flakes

½ cup soy yoghurt, to serve

½ cup chopped coriander (cilantro), to serve

Cook the onion in a large, heavy-based frying pan over medium heat until translucent. Make sure to add a bit of water if the onion begins to stick too much and take on colour. You are just looking to soften the onion at this stage and remove its raw flavour. Add the garlic and cook for 1–2 minutes until fragrant.

Add the tempeh and cook until it begins to brown, 5–8 minutes. (Keep a glass of water close by and add some, if needed.)

Add the capsicum and celery and cook until they're tender, another 5 minutes.

Add the stock, water, tomato passata, beans, oregano and spices, reduce the heat to low and simmer until the chilli is fragrant and the flavours have come together, 25–35 minutes. If the chilli mixture becomes too thick, add more water as needed.

Serve with the soy yoghurt and coriander.

Sweet potato and tempeh hash

Ingrid Adelsberger, Los Angeles, United States

Serves 4

2 sweet potatoes

1 cup diced onion

225 g (8 oz) tempeh, cut into 2.5 cm
 (1 inch) cubes

1–2 tablespoons tamari or soy sauce

1 teaspoon ground turmeric

1 teaspoon smoked paprika, or to taste

2 teaspoons dijon mustard

¼–½ cup vegetable stock, or as needed
 (homemade—for a recipe, see page 110)

3 cups tightly packed chopped kale

pinch of chilli flakes

sea salt and freshly ground black
 pepper

Preheat the oven to 200°C (400°F/gas 6).

Pierce the sweet potatoes a few times with a fork and place on a baking tray lined with baking paper. Bake for 35–45 minutes until tender but not mushy. Let cool for 15 minutes, before peeling and chopping into 1 cm (½ inch) cubes.

Cook the onion in a large, heavy-based frying pan over medium heat until translucent. Make sure to add a bit of water if the onion begins to stick too much and take on colour. You are just looking to soften the onion at this stage and remove its raw flavour.

Add the tempeh cubes and cook until they begin to brown, 5–8 minutes. (Keep a glass of water close by to add, if needed.)

Add the sweet potato, tamari or soy sauce, turmeric, smoked paprika, mustard and stock and cook for 3–5 minutes.

Stir in the kale and cook until wilted. Add the chilli flakes and season to taste.

VARIATIONS: You can microwave the sweet potatoes if time is tight. If you don't enjoy sweet potatoes or they are not available, use potatoes instead. Replace the kale with English spinach or Swiss chard.

Vegan shepherd's pie

Ingrid Adelsberger, Los Angeles, United States
Serves 4

3 potatoes, peeled and chopped
3 tablespoons plant-based milk
½ teaspoon garlic powder
sea salt and freshly ground
  black pepper
1 tablespoon extra virgin olive oil
  (optional)
flaxseed oil, to drizzle

Filling
225 g (8 oz) tempeh, chopped into
  bite-sized pieces
⅓ cup tamari or soy sauce
3 teaspoons worcestershire sauce

½ large red onion, finely chopped
3 garlic cloves, finely chopped
2 carrots, chopped
2 celery stalks, chopped
⅓ cup frozen peas
⅓ cup vegetable stock (homemade—for
  a recipe, see page 110)
3 tablespoons red wine (or more stock)
2 thyme sprigs
2 rosemary sprigs
1 teaspoon Italian seasoning
3 tablespoons wholemeal (whole-wheat)
  plain (all-purpose) flour
sea salt and freshly ground black pepper

Preheat the oven to 200°C (400°F/gas 6). Lightly oil or mist a casserole dish with extra virgin olive oil and set aside.

Place the potatoes in a large saucepan, add water and bring to the boil. Reduce the heat to low and simmer for 30 minutes until tender. Drain and return to the pan. Add the milk, garlic powder and seasoning and mash well.

In the meantime, start on the filling. Place the tempeh, tamari or soy sauce and worcestershire sauce in a heavy-based saucepan and fry for 5 minutes over medium heat. Remove from the pan.

Place the onion in the same pan and cook over medium heat until translucent. Make sure to add a bit of water if the onion begins to stick too much and take on colour. Add the garlic and dry-fry, stirring often, for 5 minutes until fragrant.

Add the carrot and celery and cook, stirring occasionally, for 10 minutes.

Add the peas, stock, red wine, herbs, Italian seasoning and flour, stir well and cook for 5–10 minutes until thickened. Season with salt and pepper, transfer to the prepared casserole dish and top with the mashed potato, brushed with the olive oil (if using).

Bake for 30–35 minutes until the topping is golden and the filling is bubbling. Let cool for 5–10 minutes, cut off a piece and drizzle with flaxseed oil.

VARIATION: You may substitute the tempeh with tofu or leave it out completely. You can also add turnips or other root vegetables (no beetroot [beets], as it will change the flavour too much).

TIP: You can omit the oil in your mashed potato if you like: just brush the top with a bit of water and it will become golden brown.

Vietnamese caramelised tofu and egg whites

Dat Nguyen, New York, United States

Serves 4

2 garlic cloves, crushed

2.5 cm (1 inch) piece of ginger, cut into strips

2½ cups water

2 tablespoons fish sauce, plus extra if needed

2 tablespoons tamari or soy sauce, plus extra if needed

400 g (14 oz) firm tofu, cut into 2.5 cm (1 inch) cubes

4–8 egg whites, hard-boiled and peeled, yolks discarded

3 tablespoons almond milk

1 teaspoon coconut extract

steamed brown rice, to serve

Caramel sauce

2 tablespoons sugar

2 tablespoons water

For the caramel sauce, combine the sugar and water in a small, heavy-based saucepan over medium heat and cook, stirring occasionally to help the sugar and water combine evenly, until the sugar melts. Continue to cook, swirling the pan, until the caramel becomes a light brown colour. Immediately remove the pan from the heat and put aside.

In a small saucepan over medium heat, sauté the garlic and ginger in 1 tablespoon of water until fragrant.

Add 1 cup of water, the fish sauce, tamari or soy sauce, tofu and egg whites. Add more water if needed to cover the egg whites—they will absorb the brown colour of the sauce—but not too much or it will dilute the sauce. Taste and add more tamari or soy sauce or fish sauce, if needed, reduce the heat to low and cook for 10 minutes.

Slowly pour about 3 tablespoons of the caramel into the pan. The more caramel added to the braise, the sweeter the flavour. Add more caramel to taste.

Pour in the almond milk and coconut extract. Simmer for half an hour to allow the tofu and egg whites to absorb the flavour.

Serve with warm rice, making sure you get lots of sauce over the rice.

NOTE: Traditionally this dish is eaten with Vietnamese pickled mustard greens, as they provide the sweet, salty and sour combination. However, if they are difficult to find, you can substitute steamed spinach.

FISH
AND
SHELLFISH

Sardine cakes

Ingrid Adelsberger, Los Angeles, United States

Makes 6

2 sweet potatoes, boiled, peeled and chopped

2 × 115 g (4 oz) cans sardines in water, drained and chopped

½ cup thinly sliced spring onions (scallions)

3 tablespoons chopped dill or 1½ tablespoons dried dill

2 tablespoons wholemeal (whole-wheat) plain (all-purpose) flour

2 garlic cloves, crushed

juice of ½ lemon

1 cup dry breadcrumbs

sea salt and freshly ground black pepper

1 egg white

Preheat the oven to 190°C (375°F/gas 5).

Boil the sweet potato until tender, 25–30 minutes, depending on the size of the pieces. Drain and mash.

Add the sardines, spring onion, dill, flour, garlic, lemon juice and breadcrumbs. Season with salt and pepper, then mix in the egg white.

Shape into six 7.5 cm (3 inch) diameter fish cakes. Place on a baking tray and bake, turning once after 15 minutes, for 25–30 minutes until lightly browned.

TIP: If you miss crab cakes, this is a great way to replace them with a healthier version, as sardines provide you with omega-3.

Sizzling trout with crushed potatoes

Hilary McCollum, Red Castle, Ireland

Serves 2

400 g (14 oz) new potatoes
4 trout fillets, skin on
sea salt and freshly ground black pepper
2 tablespoons extra virgin olive oil
5 cm (2 inch) piece of ginger, cut into matchsticks
3 garlic cloves, thinly sliced
1–2 small red chillies (to taste), deseeded and roughly chopped
2–3 tablespoons tamari or soy sauce
1 bunch of chives, snipped

Put the potatoes on to boil. They will take around 15–20 minutes, depending on their size. Drain, return the potatoes to the saucepan and cover to keep warm.

Heat your grill (broiler) to medium.

Slash the skin of each trout fillet 3–4 times. Season both sides with salt and pepper.

Put 4 drops of olive oil on a foil-lined baking tray. Spread each drop around. Place each fillet, skin side up, on the tray and put under the grill for 5 minutes. Turn and grill for 1–2 minutes until cooked to your liking.

Meanwhile, heat 1–2 tablespoons of water in a non-stick saucepan over medium–high heat. Add the ginger, garlic, chilli and tamari or soy sauce and cook for 1 minute until fragrant.

Add the chives, salt and pepper and the remaining olive oil to the potatoes. Crush roughly.

Place the trout fillets on serving plates and cover with the tamari or soy sauce, ginger, garlic and chilli mix. Add the potatoes and serve.

Cod steaks in a spicy tomato sauce

Sue Collis, Winchester, United Kingdom

Serves 4

1½ teaspoons sea salt

½ teaspoon cayenne pepper

¼ teaspoon ground turmeric

4 × 250 g (9 oz) cod steaks, thawed if frozen, patted dry

1 teaspoon fennel seeds

1 teaspoon mustard seeds

175 g (6 oz) onions, finely chopped

2 garlic cloves, crushed

2 teaspoons ground cumin

500 g (1 lb 2 oz) tomato passata

¼ teaspoon garam masala

steamed long-grain brown rice, to serve

Mix together the salt, cayenne pepper and turmeric, and rub into the fish steaks. Leave to marinate for 30 minutes.

Heat a saucepan over medium heat, add the fennel seeds and mustard seeds and stir for a few seconds until they start to pop. Reduce the heat to medium–low, add the onion and garlic and cook for 3–5 minutes, stirring a few times. Add a little water if the mixture starts to stick.

Stir in the ground cumin, add the passata and garam masala, stir to mix. Bring to the boil, turn down the heat to low and simmer for 15 minutes.

Sear the fish on both sides in a frying pan lined with baking paper; do not use oil.

Add the fish to the saucepan, nestling it into the tomato sauce. Continue to simmer until the fish is cooked through, about 5 minutes. If the sauce thickens too much, it can be loosened with boiling water, stirred in. Serve with rice.

NOTE: This recipe also works with prawns, vegetables and using a standard oil-free curry powder instead of individual spices.

Salmon in chraimeh sauce

Molly Greenwood, London, United Kingdom

Serves 2

2 onions, peeled
6 garlic cloves, peeled
1 small green chilli
2 teaspoons sweet paprika
1 tablespoon caraway seeds, toasted and ground
1½ teaspoons ground cumin
⅓ teaspoon cayenne pepper
⅓ teaspoon ground cinnamon
150 ml (5 fl oz) water
3 tablespoons tomato purée
2 teaspoons caster (superfine) sugar
juice of 1 large lemon, plus extra to serve
sea salt and freshly ground black pepper
2 salmon fillets or steaks, pin-boned
2 tablespoons extra virgin olive oil (optional)
2 tablespoons roughly chopped coriander (cilantro)
steamed short-grain brown rice, to serve
2 handfuls of steamed broccoli stems, to serve

Place the onions, garlic, chilli and spices in a food processor and blitz into a thick paste.

Heat a frying pan over medium heat and add 1–2 tablespoons of water, then add the spice paste and stir for 30 seconds. Add the remaining water and the tomato purée, bring to a simmer and stir in the sugar and lemon juice.

Season well, add the fish and spoon over the sauce to cover. Put the lid on and simmer gently for 7–11 minutes until the fish is just done.

Drizzle with the olive oil (if using), sprinkle with the coriander and an extra squeeze of lemon, if you fancy, and serve with rice and some lightly steamed tender stem broccoli.

Herring in oats

Jill Pack, London, United Kingdom

Serves 2

2 tablespoons extra virgin olive oil
⅔ cup plain (all-purpose) flour
2 egg whites
150 g (5½ oz) rolled (porridge) oats
sea salt and freshly ground black pepper
4 herring fillets

Preheat the oven to 180°C (350°F/gas 4) or 160°C (315°F/gas 2–3) fan-forced. Lightly grease a baking tin with a little extra virgin olive oil.

Prepare three shallow bowls—one with the flour, one with the egg whites and finally one with the oats seasoned with salt and lots of pepper.

Dip each herring fillet in the flour, then in the egg white, then in the oats until both sides are well covered. Place carefully in the prepared tin, making sure the fish is not overlapping. Drizzle the rest of the olive oil over the fish and bake for 30 minutes until crisp and brown.

TIP: Serve this dish with crushed potatoes mixed with flaxseed oil, and carrots and a green vegetable. A great meal for those who used to love 'meat and two veg'.

Baked stuffed mackerel

Jill Pack, London, United Kingdom

Serves 4

1 small onion, finely chopped
1 tablespoon oatmeal
1 cup fresh wholemeal (whole-wheat) breadcrumbs
2 teaspoons chopped lemon thyme
3 teaspoons chopped flat-leaf (Italian) parsley
sea salt and freshly ground black pepper
2–3 tablespoons hot water, if required
4 whole mackerel, cleaned, gutted and washed thoroughly

Preheat the oven to 180°C (350°F/gas 4) or 160°C (315°F/gas 2–3) fan-forced.

Cook the onion in a heavy-based frying pan over medium heat until translucent. Make sure to add a bit of water if the onion begins to stick too much and take on colour. You are just looking to soften the onion at this stage and remove its raw flavour.

Add the oatmeal, breadcrumbs, herbs and seasoning to the softened onion and mix well to form a firm stuffing. Add a little hot water to bind, if necessary.

Fill the cavities of the fish with the stuffing and wrap each one separately in baking paper to form a closed parcel. Place each fish parcel on a baking tray and bake for half an hour. Before serving, remove the fish from the baking paper.

Miso mackerel (saba no miso ni)

Carl Herring, Setagaya-ku, Hanegi, Japan

Serves 2

2 large mackerel fillets, skin on
1 tablespoon soft brown sugar
3 tablespoons sake
2–3 tablespoons mirin
1 tablespoon tamari or soy sauce
1 thumb-sized piece of ginger, sliced into thin strips, plus extra to garnish
2–3 tablespoons miso paste (red or white, or a mixture of both)
steamed brown rice and green salad, to serve

Cut each mackerel fillet into three roughly equal pieces, each about 5 cm (2 inches) wide.

Put about 1 cm (½ inch) of water into a large saucepan. Add the sugar, sake, mirin, tamari or soy sauce and ginger and bring to the boil. Immediately reduce the heat to low.

Take a small amount of the sake mixture and use it to dissolve the miso paste in a separate bowl.

Stir the dissolved miso into the pan and add the mackerel pieces, skin side up. Rest a lid from a smaller pan directly on the mackerel pieces (this stops them breaking up and helps them to absorb the sauce. Traditionally, the Japanese use an *otoshibuta* (drop lid) for this, but a small pan lid also works well). Cook for 8 minutes, but don't let it boil.

Carefully lift the mackerel pieces onto plates and spoon over the sauce. Top with the extra ginger slivers and serve with rice and green salad.

Hoisin mackerel

Jill Pack, London, United Kingdom

Serves 4

4 mackerel fillets
1 small red chilli, deseeded, if desired, and chopped
1 walnut-sized piece of ginger, cut into matchsticks
3 tablespoons hoisin sauce (OMS-friendly)
2 tablespoons honey
2 tablespoons tamari or soy sauce
2 tablespoons rice wine or dry sherry

Lay the fish fillets in a shallow ovenproof dish.

Put the chilli and ginger in a small bowl, stir in the hoisin sauce, honey, tamari or soy sauce and rice wine or dry sherry. Pour the marinade over the fish and leave for an hour or more in a cool place.

Preheat the oven to 200°C (400°F/gas 6) or 180°C (350°F/gas 4) fan-forced. Bake the fish with the marinade for 20 minutes until the sauce is bubbling. It helps to keep the fish moist if you spoon the marinade over the fish after 10–15 minutes.

TIP: If you're not a great fan of mackerel, try it with a gooseberry sauce. Just cook some gooseberries with a bit of sugar and let the sauce cool (try frozen if they are out of season or even just mash the gooseberries from a tin). The tartness of the gooseberries cuts through the oiliness of the fish that some find unctuous.

Creole-inspired salmon

Victoria Riches, Norfolk, United Kingdom

Serves 2

2 chunky salmon fillets, 140 g (5 oz) each, pin-boned and skinned

Seasoning

1 dessertspoon sweet paprika

1 teaspoon dried oregano

1 teaspoon dried thyme

¾ teaspoon garlic powder

⅓ teaspoon sea salt

¼ teaspoon cayenne pepper

½ teaspoon black pepper

Preheat the oven to 220°C (425°F/gas 7).

Mix the seasoning ingredients together in a shallow bowl. Coat the salmon fillets in the seasoning mix and leave to marinate for 15 minutes.

Place the salmon on a baking tray, cover with foil and bake in the middle of the oven for 10 minutes (adjust the cooking time according to preference and the thickness of the fillets).

TIP: Delicious served with a fresh salad or potato wedges and steamed vegetables.

Gravlax

Linda Bloom, London, United Kingdom

Serves 2–3 (depending on size of salmon)

Gravlax must be made 48 hours prior to use, and will keep well in the fridge for a week.

50 g (1¾ oz) coarse rock salt

1 teaspoon sugar

1 teaspoon freshly ground black pepper

1½ bunches of dill, chopped, plus extra to serve

1 side of salmon, filleted, skin on, pin-boned and sides trimmed

1–2 tablespoons extra virgin olive oil, plus extra to serve

2 tablespoons cognac, gin or vodka

lemon wedges, to serve

Combine the rock salt, sugar and pepper in a bowl.

Cover the base of a large glass dish with half the dill. Rub the flesh of the salmon with the olive oil and place, skin side down, on the bed of dill. Evenly spread the rock salt mixture over the salmon, then cover with the remaining dill. Sprinkle over the cognac, gin or vodka. Place a foil-covered, stiff cardboard shape, which has been cut to fit the dish, over the fish and weigh it down with weights—say two 400 g (14 oz) cans of tomatoes. Refrigerate for 24 hours.

Turn the salmon over, pour off some of the excess liquid collected in the dish, cover, weigh down as before and return to the refrigerator for another 24 hours.

After a total of 48 hours, wash off the salt and dill mixture and dry the salmon with paper towel. It is now ready to use. Keep wrapped in foil in the fridge for 3–5 days. Slice thinly as for smoked salmon and serve with lemon, best-quality olive oil and dill.

Salmon kedgeree

Lucie Williams, Paraparaumu, New Zealand
Serves 6

2 generous cups frozen peas
1 head of broccoli, cut into florets
1 bunch of spring onions (scallions), white and green part thinly sliced
2 teaspoons curry powder
3 cups basmati rice, cooked and cooled
300 g (10½ oz) hot-smoked salmon, flaked
chopped flat-leaf (Italian) parsley and lemon juice, to serve (optional)
2–3 teaspoons extra virgin olive oil

Bring a large saucepan of water to the boil and add the peas. When the water starts boiling again, add the broccoli and bring to the boil. Cook for 3 minutes, then drain. Set aside.

Fry the spring onion in 1 tablespoon of water in a heavy-based saucepan over medium heat for 10 minutes, stirring regularly.

Stir in the curry powder, increase the heat to high and cook for 1 minute until fragrant.

Add the rice and stir to coat (it should be yellow all over). Lower the heat to medium.

Gently stir in the salmon, peas and broccoli. Serve immediately with the parsley and lemon juice and a drizzle of olive oil.

 It pays to read labels! I find that the saturated fats in hot-smoked salmon vary enormously, depending on the brand.

Lucie Williams, Paraparaumu, New Zealand

Salmon flatbread

Claire Donkin, Ballsgate Cottage, United Kingdom
Serves 1

1 pita bread round
1–2 tablespoons tomato passata or salsa (for a homemade salsa recipe, see page 231)

Toppings to mix and match
capers, sliced olives, sliced tomato, sliced onion
1–2 slices smoked salmon
chilli flakes
leafy salad, to serve

Split the pita in half and cover each piece with the passata or salsa. Add the capers, olives, tomato and onion. Top with the salmon and add a pinch of chilli flakes. Grill (broil) until the smoked salmon is hot. Serve with a big leafy salad.

TIP: This is like a pizza, but without the bother of making the dough—a quick, delicious lunch.

Marinated salmon

Abba Renshaw, Auckland, New Zealand

Serves 4

1 bunch of coriander (cilantro)
2 tablespoons Lemongrass Paste (see recipe, page 221)
2 garlic cloves, finely chopped
2 tablespoons finely chopped ginger
4 salmon tail fillets, pin-boned
1 cup tamari or soy sauce
juice of 2 limes
1 bunch of spring onions (scallions), finely chopped
boiled potatoes and salad, to serve

Separate the coriander leaves from the stems and finely chop the stems.

Combine the lemongrass paste, coriander stems, garlic and ginger in a bowl to make a paste.

Rub the paste on the salmon and place the salmon in a shallow dish, in a single layer, with the skin side up. Pour over the tamari or soy sauce to almost cover the salmon. Marinate in the fridge for 1 hour.

Preheat the oven to 180°C (350°F/gas 4).

Remove the salmon from the marinade, place on a baking tray and drizzle on some of the marinade. Bake for 8–12 minutes, depending on the thickness of the fillets and how you like your salmon. Sprinkle on the lime juice, coriander leaves and spring onion and serve with boiled potatoes and salad.

Baked salmon in maple mustard sauce

Ingrid Adelsberger, Los Angeles, United States
Serves 2

2 × 175 g (6 oz) salmon fillets, pin-boned
1 tablespoon maple syrup
1 teaspoon dijon mustard
1 teaspoon balsamic vinegar
sea salt and freshly ground black pepper
steamed brown rice and a salad or steamed vegetables, to serve

Preheat the oven to 180°C (350°F/gas 4). Line a baking tray with foil or baking paper.

Place the salmon on the prepared tray. Mix the maple syrup, dijon mustard, balsamic vinegar, salt and pepper in a small bowl, then drizzle over the salmon. Bake for 10–12 minutes until the crust is lightly golden. Serve with rice and a salad or steamed vegetables.

Salmon parcels

Denise Liesch, Herne Hill, Australia

Serves 2

2 spring onions (scallions), chopped

2 frozen salmon fillets, thawed, skin removed and pin-boned

1 teaspoon grated ginger

1 long red chilli, deseeded and finely chopped

1 lime, cut into 6 slices

1 bunch of coriander (cilantro), roughly chopped

2 teaspoons tamari or soy sauce

1 teaspoon mirin

steamed brown rice and steamed vegetables or a salad, to serve

Preheat the oven to 200°C (400°F/gas 6).

Prepare the parcels by taking two 30 cm (12 inch) pieces of foil and lining them with baking paper. Place half the spring onion in the centre of each, then add a salmon fillet and half the ginger, chilli, lime slices and coriander in a stack. Mix together the tamari or soy sauce and mirin before pouring the sauce over the fish. Wrap each parcel by bringing the top and bottom sides together and folding over a couple of times, then rolling up each end.

Bake for 10–12 minutes or until the salmon is cooked through. (If you like your salmon raw in the centre, cut the baking time.) You'll be greeted with amazing smells when you open the parcels—absolutely delicious. Serve with rice and vegetables or a salad of your choice.

Baked crusted cod

Lyn Welch, London, United Kingdom

Serves 2

2 cod steaks
steamed vegetables or salad, to serve

Crust
about ⅓ cup fresh breadcrumbs
1 good handful of chopped flat-leaf (Italian) parsley
finely grated zest of ½ lemon
6 sun-dried tomatoes, chopped (I use those marinated in olive oil and
   squeeze the oil out)
1 sprinkle of smoked paprika
sea salt and freshly ground black pepper

Preheat the oven to 180°C (350°F/gas 4).

Mix together all the crust ingredients.

Place the cod in an ovenproof dish. Spoon the breadcrumb mixture over the top of each cod steak and gently press into the flesh. If some spills over just press it onto the side. Bake for about 20 minutes. Serve with vegetables or your salad of choice.

TIP: This crust can be used on any fish. It works well on salmon, as the breadcrumbs absorb the oil.

Calamari with turmeric and garlic

Andree, Dromana, Australia

Gluten-free • Serves 4

8 medium or 16 small cleaned squid tubes, cut into bite-sized pieces

1 avocado, cubed

½ bunch coriander (cilantro), chopped

juice of ½ lime

½ cup water or fat-free fish stock, plus extra

3 tablespoons white wine

2 teaspoons grated fresh turmeric or 1 teaspoon ground turmeric

2 teaspoons finely grated ginger

2 garlic cloves mashed with ½ teaspoon Himalayan salt or sea salt

Place the squid in a small bowl and set aside.

Combine the avocado, coriander and lime juice in a bowl and set aside for 15 minutes.

Place the water or stock in a saucepan. Add the wine, turmeric, ginger and garlic. Simmer for 2–3 minutes until the garlic, ginger and turmeric are cooked through.

Add the squid, 8–10 pieces at a time, and simmer, turning after 30–40 seconds, for 1–2 minutes only, then transfer to a bowl. Repeat this process until all the squid is cooked, adding more water or stock to the pan to top up as needed. Continue to cook the sauce until thickened and reduced. Use this sauce as a dressing over the squid and serve with a salad and the avocado salsa.

TIP: Add the squid and dressing hot or cold to salads, or add it hot to rice and beans or pasta. Make sure to drizzle the sauce over your preferred dish.

Chilli and tomato fish

Jo, Freshwater, Australia

Serves 4

4–5 firm white fish fillets (Spanish mackerel is good), chopped into bite-sized pieces
juice of 2 limes
coriander (cilantro), to serve
steamed brown rice, to serve

Sauce
2 French shallots
2 garlic cloves
500 g (1 lb 2 oz) tomatoes, chopped
1 tablespoon tomato purée
2 small red chillies, finely chopped
2 teaspoons sugar or honey
4 cm (1½ inch) piece of ginger, grated or finely chopped
3 teaspoons garam masala
1 dessertspoon tamari or soy sauce
sea salt

To make the sauce, cook the shallot in a little water until soft, add the garlic and cook until softened. Add all the other ingredients and simmer until you have a nice rich sauce. Taste! Don't worry if it is a bit sweet, as lime juice is to come.

Add the fish to the sauce and simmer until cooked through. Stir in the lime juice and adjust the seasoning to taste. Sprinkle the coriander over the top and serve with rice.

TIP: This dish is yummy but tastes ho-hum if you don't add the lime juice at the end.

Saag prawns

Rae Jackman, Fife, Scotland

Serves 4

2 large onions, extremely finely chopped
2.5 cm (1 inch) piece of ginger, finely grated
5 garlic cloves, finely chopped
400 g (14 oz) can crushed tomatoes
½ teaspoon sea salt
½ teaspoon cayenne pepper
1 teaspoon ground coriander
½ teaspoon ground turmeric
2 cloves
1 teaspoon garam masala
2 cardamom pods
200 g (7 oz) English spinach leaves, chopped
400 g (14 oz) frozen raw prawns (shrimp), thawed

Cook the onion in a heavy-based frying pan over medium heat until translucent. If the onion begins to stick too much and take on colour, add a bit of water. You just want to soften the onion at this stage and remove its raw flavour. Add the ginger and garlic and cook, stirring occasionally, for a few minutes until fragrant.

Add the tomatoes, salt, cayenne pepper, coriander, turmeric, cloves, garam masala and cardamom and simmer gently until tender, about 5–7 minutes.

Steam the spinach until just wilted, 2–3 minutes, and add to the curry base with the prawns. Simmer until the prawns are just cooked through, about 5 minutes. Don't overcook.

TIP: I find cooking the onion, garlic and spices for longer over a very low heat enhances the flavour.

Thai prawns

Hester Dekker, Vught, The Netherlands

Serves 4

1 bunch of coriander (cilantro)
4 garlic cloves, chopped
1 tablespoon white peppercorns
4 anchovy fillets (optional)
1 tablespoon brown rice vinegar (optional)
2 tablespoons soft brown sugar
1–2 tablespoons fish sauce
1 tablespoon light tamari or light soy sauce
1 small green chilli, chopped (optional)
16 raw large prawns (shrimp), peeled and deveined with tails intact
steamed rice, salad and lime wedges, to serve

Trim about 3–4 cm (1¼–1½ inches) from the root end of the coriander. Rinse the roots, then finely chop them and put them into a mortar. Roughly chop the coriander leaves and stems and set aside.

Add the garlic and peppercorns to the coriander roots and pound to a paste with a pestle, then mash the anchovy fillets with brown rice vinegar (if using).

Scrape the paste and anchovy mixture (if using) into a bowl, then stir in the brown sugar, fish sauce, tamari or soy sauce and chilli. Add the prawns and toss to coat in the paste. Set aside at room temperature for 30 minutes, or cover and refrigerate for 3–6 hours.

Half an hour before cooking, remove the prawns from the fridge. Heat a frying pan over high heat. Add the prawns and marinade and cook for 2 minutes on each side until pink. Don't overcook! Serve with rice or a salad and lime wedges on the side and garnish with the coriander leaves.

Prawn and pea egg white frittata

Debbie Scrivens, West Sussex, United Kingdom

Serves 4

100 g (3½ oz) couscous

8 spring onions (scallions), sliced

150 ml (5 fl oz) boiling water

10 large egg whites (400 g [14 oz] free-range egg whites in supermarket chiller cabinet)

250 g (9 oz) cooked peeled prawns (shrimp)

250 g (9 oz) frozen peas, thawed

4 sun-dried tomatoes (not in oil), chopped

1 teaspoon dried oregano

sea salt and freshly ground black pepper

dried chilli flakes or Tabasco sauce (if you like it spicy)

flaxseed oil, to drizzle on top (optional)

Preheat the oven to 180°C (350°F/gas 4). Line a small roasting tin with baking paper.

Place the couscous and spring onion in a bowl and pour over the water. Cover and set aside for 5 minutes.

Beat the egg whites to stiff peaks, stir in the prawns, peas, tomatoes, oregano, salt and pepper, and dried chilli flakes or Tabasco (if using).

Fluff up the couscous with a fork and mix into the egg white mixture. Pour into the prepared tin and bake for 30–35 minutes until set and browned on top. Keep an eye on it to make sure it doesn't burn! Drizzle with a little flaxseed oil if you like. The frittata can be eaten hot or cold.

***

VARIATION: Use asparagus or leeks and salmon instead of peas and prawns, or try cooked spinach, zucchini (courgette), mushroom and capsicum (bell pepper).

Fish lasagne

Silvia Gautschi McNulty, Zurich, Switzerland

Serves 6–8

3–4 eggplants (aubergines), cut lengthways into 1 cm (½ inch) thick slices

enough dried thyme to lightly coat each eggplant

sea salt

olive oil

6–8 white fish fillets (about 120 g [4¼ oz] each)

freshly ground black pepper

about 500 g (1 lb 2 oz) tomato passata

about 2 cups Vegan Béchamel Sauce (see recipe, page 214)

dried lasagne sheets

about 5 tablespoons nutritional yeast

Preheat the oven to 180°C (350°F/gas 4).

Season the eggplant with the thyme, salt and a light coating of olive oil.

Heat a chargrill pan over medium–high heat and grill (broil) the eggplant until well marked on both sides and softened. Reserve.

Lightly season the fish fillets with salt and pepper. Place in a steamer and cook for 2–3 minutes until half cooked. Be careful to avoid cooking too much as it will dry out in the lasagne. Reserve.

Heat the tomato passata and béchamel sauce in separate saucepans. Now, begin constructing the lasagne by placing a ladle of béchamel sauce on the bottom of your baking dish—I use a 25 × 30 cm (10 × 12 inch) dish. Add a layer of pasta sheets, cover with a layer of eggplant, then top with one-third of the warm tomato passata. Add another light coating of béchamel, then another layer of pasta sheets, followed by half the remaining tomato passata and the fish fillets. Add a final layer of pasta sheets, then top with the remaining tomato passata.

Combine the remaining béchamel with the nutritional yeast and smooth over the top of the lasagne. Bake for 25 minutes until a knife can be easily inserted through the pasta sheets. Cool slightly, brush with olive oil and enjoy right away.

Fish tacos

Ingrid Adelsberger, Los Angeles, United States

Serves 4

3 tablespoons soy yoghurt

2 tablespoons chopped coriander (cilantro)

2 tablespoons lime juice

1 jalapeno chilli, deseeded and chopped

1 cup thinly sliced onion

1½ teaspoons sweet paprika

1½ teaspoons soft brown sugar

1 teaspoon dried oregano

¾ teaspoon garlic powder

½ teaspoon sea salt

¼ teaspoon chilli powder

½ teaspoon ground cumin

4 × 175 g (6 oz) white fish fillets (such as tilapia, whiting or snapper)

½ ripe avocado, thinly sliced

8 × 15 cm (6 inch) corn tortillas (make sure they are OMS-friendly), warmed

4 lime wedges

½ cup salsa (optional—for a homemade recipe, see page 231)

2 cups cooked long-grain brown rice (optional)

Place the soy yoghurt, coriander, lime juice and chilli in a food processor and process until smooth. Transfer to a small bowl and mix in the onion.

Combine the paprika, sugar, oregano, garlic powder, salt, chilli powder and cumin in a separate bowl, mix well and sprinkle evenly over the fish.

Heat a frying pan over medium heat and add 1 tablespoon of water and the fish and cook for 3 minutes on each side, or until it is cooked (keep a glass of water close and add if needed).

Divide the fish, chilli and onion mixture and the avocado evenly among the tortillas. Serve with the lime wedges and, if desired, the salsa and rice.

VEGETABLES

Mexican stuffed portobello mushrooms

Ashley Madden, St John's, Canada

Gluten-free • Serves 4

½ onion, finely chopped

2 garlic cloves, finely chopped

1 red capsicum (bell pepper), finely diced

4 large portobello mushrooms, stems removed and finely chopped

2 teaspoons chilli powder

1 teaspoon ground cumin

1½ cups cooked long-grain brown rice

½ cup black beans (canned is fine)

½ cup frozen or canned corn kernels

½ cup salsa (medium heat), plus extra (for a homemade recipe, see page 231)

juice of ½ lime

1 teaspoon sea salt

1 avocado, sliced

Preheat the oven to 180°C (350°F/gas 4).

Cook the onion in a large, heavy-based frying pan over medium heat until translucent. Make sure to add a bit of water if the onion begins to stick too much and take on colour. You are just looking to soften the onion at this stage and remove its raw flavour. Add the garlic and dry-fry for 3–5 minutes.

Add the capsicum, mushroom stems, chilli powder and cumin and sauté until the capsicum is softened, 5–7 minutes.

Add the rice, black beans, corn and salsa and cook for 7–10 minutes. Stir in the lime juice. Taste and adjust with salt, if necessary.

Fill each mushroom cap with the rice and bean mixture (there will be some left over) and top with another tablespoon of salsa. Transfer to a baking dish, cover with foil and bake for 15 minutes. Remove the foil and bake for another 10 minutes.

Top each mushroom with the avocado slices (a dollop of guacamole would be even better!).

VARIATION: Additional toppings could be diced tomatoes or thinly sliced spring onions (scallions).

Potato quinoa patties with chickpea curry

Alexandra, Johannesburg, South Africa

Serves 6

3 potatoes, boiled and mashed

1–1½ cups cooked quinoa

⅓ red onion, finely chopped

1 small green chilli, finely chopped

1 tablespoon chopped ginger

½ teaspoon cumin seeds

½ teaspoon chilli powder

1 teaspoon ground coriander

sea salt

2 tablespoons coarsely ground rolled (porridge) oats

Chickpea curry

2 tomatoes, chopped

2.5 cm (1 inch) piece of ginger, chopped

1 small green chilli

2 garlic cloves

½ teaspoon sea salt

½ teaspoon cumin seeds

½ teaspoon mustard seeds

1 onion, chopped

10 curry leaves

½ teaspoon ground coriander

½ teaspoon garam masala

¼–½ teaspoon cayenne pepper

¼ teaspoon ground turmeric

1 cup dried chickpeas (garbanzo beans), soaked overnight in water, drained

4 cups water

I start by making the chickpea curry in a pressure cooker. Blend the tomatoes, ginger, chilli, garlic and salt into a purée and set aside.

Toast the cumin and mustard seeds in a separate pan and cook until they start to pop. Set aside.

Cook the onion in a wide heavy-based saucepan over medium heat until translucent. Make sure to add a bit of water if the onion begins to stick too much and take on colour. Stir in the toasted seeds, curry leaves and spices. Add the blended tomato mixture and cook, stirring occasionally, until it thickens a bit, 4–5 minutes.

Add the chickpeas and water and cook for 28 minutes after the pressure reaches the second bar. Add the tomatoes, taste and adjust salt and spices. Then gently release the pressure by running cold water over the top and sides of the pressure cooker, otherwise the chickpeas will overcook.

Preheat the oven to 180°C (350°F/gas 4) and prepare the potato quinoa patties.

In a large bowl, combine the potato with the rest of the ingredients and mix well. Shape into patties and bake on a lined baking tray for 15–20 minutes.

To serve, spoon some chickpea curry onto serving plates and top with the patties.

Indian-spiced chickpeas

Catherine Street, Altrincham, United Kingdom

Gluten-free • Serves 3

1 onion, chopped
2 garlic cloves, finely chopped
¾ teaspoon ground coriander
1 teaspoon ground cumin
425 g (15 oz) can chickpeas (garbanzo beans), undrained
3 tomatoes, puréed, or ⅔ cup tomato passata
½ teaspoon curry powder
¼ teaspoon ground turmeric
¼ teaspoon sea salt
1 tablespoon lemon juice
1 bunch of English spinach leaves
steamed brown rice or another whole grain, to serve

Cook the onion in a large, heavy-based saucepan over medium heat until translucent. Make sure to add a bit of water if the onion begins to stick too much and take on colour. You are just looking to soften the onion at this stage and remove its raw flavour. Add the garlic and sauté until soft, about 2 minutes.

Reduce the heat to medium–low and add the coriander and cumin and stir for 1 minute.

Add the chickpeas and the liquid in the can, the tomato purée or passata, curry powder, turmeric and salt and simmer, stirring occasionally, until most of the liquid has been absorbed, 10–12 minutes.

Add the lemon juice and spinach, stir to combine and cook just until the spinach begins to wilt, about 1 minute. Serve immediately with rice or another grain.

 TIP: For extra heat, add a dash of cayenne pepper before serving.

Stuffed capsicums

Pam Schartner, Tranmere, Australia

Serves 6

1 small onion or 6 spring onions (scallions), finely chopped

1 cup vegetable stock (homemade—for a recipe, see page 110)

4 garlic cloves, finely chopped

2 small zucchini (courgettes), finely chopped, or ½ cup chopped seasonal vegetables (such as summer squash, corn kernels)

3 tablespoons dried red lentils

1 small red chilli, chopped (optional)

3 tablespoons wholemeal (whole-wheat) risoni or long-grain brown rice

12 button mushrooms, chopped

1 generous handful of silverbeet (Swiss chard) or baby spinach leaves

6 tomatoes

8 basil leaves

6 fat-bottomed green or red capsicums (bell peppers)

salad, to serve

This was my first OMS recipe in 1999 that I adapted from the meaty version of stuffed capsicums.

Preheat the oven to 180°C (350°F/gas 4).

Soften the onion or spring onion in 1 tablespoon of stock in a frying pan over low heat, then add the garlic. Add the zucchini or seasonal vegetables and cook until softened. Stir in the lentils, chilli, risoni or rice and the remaining stock and cook gently for 15 minutes until most of the stock is absorbed. Add the mushrooms and silverbeet or spinach and cook for a few minutes more. Remove from the heat and allow to cool for a few minutes.

While that is cooking, toss the tomatoes and basil in a blender and blend.

Carefully remove the stalk, seeds and membrane from the capsicums, making as small a hole in the top as possible. Carefully stuff each capsicum with the vegetable mixture and place, upright, in an ovenproof dish. Spoon over any remaining vegetable mixture, then pour on the puréed tomato.

Bake for 30–40 minutes until the capsicums soften. Serve with a salad.

TIP: If the puréed tomatoes are a bit thick, pour over a few tablespoons of no added salt tomato juice (such as V8).

Sweet and sour haricot beans

Andrea Mitson, Derbyshire, United Kingdom

Serves 4

1 onion, chopped
2 red capsicums (bell peppers), chopped
1 garlic clove
1 × 300 g (10½ oz) can apricots in juice
2 tablespoons red wine vinegar
2 tablespoons tomato purée or tomato passata
1 tablespoon tamari or soy sauce
2 teaspoons honey
2 tablespoons cornflour (cornstarch)
2 cups vegetable stock (homemade—for a recipe, see page 110)
1 × 400 g (14 oz) can haricot beans
250 g (9 oz) button mushrooms, chopped
400 g (14 oz) can diced tomatoes
pinch of sea salt and freshly ground black pepper

Cook the onion, capsicum and garlic in a heavy-based frying pan over medium heat until softened. Make sure to add a bit of water if the vegetables begin to stick too much and take on colour.

To make the sauce, strain the apricot juice into a bowl, reserve the apricots, and mix in the red wine vinegar, tomato purée or passata, tamari or soy sauce and honey. Dissolve the cornflour in a little of the stock, then add to the sauce.

Add the remaining stock and the sauce to the onion mixture. Add the reserved apricots, haricot beans, mushrooms and diced tomatoes, season and simmer for up to 45 minutes until the sauce has cooked with the other ingredients.

TIPS: This is a quick and easy meal that uses many pantry staples. Serve with rice or rice noodles and a dash of tamari or soy sauce.

If you don't have canned apricots, soak dried ones in water and use that. It won't be as sweet as the apricot juice from the can.

Spicy sweet potato pasties

Geoff Allix, Devon, United Kingdom

Makes 4–6

400 g (14 oz) plain (all-purpose) flour
pinch of sea salt
75 ml (2¼ fl oz) extra virgin olive oil
½ cup cold water
1 onion, chopped
2 sweet potatoes, chopped
1 parsnip, chopped
2 teaspoons curry powder
sea salt and freshly ground black pepper
1 teaspoon ground cumin
1 teaspoon ground turmeric
½ teaspoon chilli flakes (optional)

Preheat the oven to 170°C (325°F/gas 3).

Combine the flour and salt in a bowl. Add the olive oil and mix with a fork until crumbly. Add the water a bit at a time and mix to form a dough. Wrap the dough in plastic wrap and put in the fridge for 30 minutes.

Mix together the onion, sweet potato, parsnip, curry powder, salt and pepper, cumin, turmeric and chilli flakes (if using).

Divide the dough into 4–6 balls (depending on the size you like). Roll each dough ball into a circle. Add the filling to one side of the circle and fold over the other half to make a semicircle. Brush the edge with water and press to seal each pasty. Cut two small holes on the top to allow the steam to escape. Bake for 30–40 minutes until golden.

Sweet potato falafels

Sarah Cook, Surrey, United Kingdom

Makes 12

2 sweet potatoes (around 700 g [1 lb 9 oz] in total)
2 spring onions (scallions), chopped
1½ teaspoons ground cumin
2 small garlic cloves, chopped
1½ teaspoons ground coriander
2 large handfuls of coriander (cilantro), chopped
juice of ½ lemon
chilli flakes (optional)
1 cup chickpea flour (besan), plus extra
sea salt and freshly ground black pepper
sprinkle of sesame seeds

Preheat the oven to 180°C (350°F/gas 4) and roast the sweet potatoes until just tender, 30–60 minutes (depending on size). Remove from the oven, leave the sweet potatoes to cool, then peel.

Put the sweet potato, spring onion, cumin, garlic, ground and fresh coriander, lemon juice, chilli flakes (if using) and chickpea flour into a large bowl. Season well and mash until smooth. Place in the fridge to firm up for an hour, or in the freezer for 20–30 minutes. When you take it out, your mix should be sticky rather than really wet. You can add a tablespoon or so more of chickpea flour, if necessary (the water content of sweet potatoes varies enormously).

Reheat the oven to 180°C (350°F/gas 4). Using a couple of soup spoons, put a well-heaped spoonful of mixture in one spoon and use the concave side of the other to shape the sides, then put them on a baking tray lined with baking paper. They should look like falafel. Sprinkle some sesame seeds on top and bake for around 20 minutes until the bases are golden brown.

TIP: If time is tight, microwave the sweet potatoes.

Sweet potato and brussels sprout gratin

Ingrid Adelsberger, Los Angeles, United States

Serves 4

extra virgin olive oil, for brushing

3 tablespoons diced French shallots

3 cups shredded brussels sprouts

sea salt and freshly ground black pepper

3 tablespoons dried cranberries

2 sweet potatoes, grated

Almond cream sauce

⅓ cup almonds

1 cup vegetable stock (homemade—for a recipe, see page 110)

1 tablespoon maple syrup

2 large garlic cloves, crushed

1 tablespoon nutritional yeast

Preheat the oven to 180°C (350°F/gas 4). Brush a cast-iron, oven-proof frying pan with olive oil.

Fry the shallot in 1 tablespoon of water for 3–4 minutes until fragrant. Add the brussels sprouts, season with salt and pepper and cook, stirring frequently, for 3 minutes until almost cooked through. Transfer to a bowl, add the dried cranberries, toss to combine and set aside.

Meanwhile, combine all the sauce ingredients in a high-speed blender and whiz until creamy, about 2 minutes. Set aside.

Place a layer of sweet potato in the prepared frying pan, cover with a layer of almond cream sauce and then top with a layer of the brussels sprout and cranberry mixture. Finish with a layer of the remaining sweet potato and top with the remaining almond cream sauce. Cover the pan with foil and bake for 40 minutes.

Remove the foil and bake for 5–10 minutes until the sweet potato is brown. Let cool for at least 5 minutes, then serve.

Mexican stuffed squash

Ashley Madden, St John's, Canada

Gluten-free • Serves 2

1 acorn squash or small butternut pumpkin
1 onion, finely diced
2 garlic cloves, finely chopped
1 red capsicum (bell pepper), finely diced
1 cup finely chopped cauliflower
1 teaspoon chilli powder
1 teaspoon ground cumin
1 cup frozen corn kernels
1 cup beans (such as black beans, chickpeas [garbanzo beans], romano beans)
1¼ cups cooked quinoa
½ cup salsa (homemade—for a recipe, see page 231)
1 avocado, sliced

Preheat the oven to 200°C (400°F/gas 6). Line a baking tray with baking paper.

Cut the squash or pumpkin (if using) in half, scoop out the middle and pierce the back of each half three to four times with a knife. Place both halves of the squash, cut side down, on the prepared tray. Bake for 30–40 minutes (depending on the size of the squash) until the outside gives a little when you press on it. Remove from the oven and set aside.

Meanwhile, combine the onion, garlic, capsicum and cauliflower in a saucepan over medium heat and sauté in 1–2 tablespoons of water for 2–3 minutes, adding more water as necessary to prevent burning.

Add the spices and continue to cook until the onion is translucent, 5 minutes.

Add the corn, beans and quinoa and continue to cook, stirring and adding water as needed to prevent burning, for another 5 minutes.

Divide the onion mixture in half (you will likely have leftover filling), flip the squash halves over and add the filling to each scooped-out portion. Top each half with 3 tablespoons of salsa and return to the oven to bake for 10 minutes. Remove from the oven, top with avocado slices and the remaining salsa and serve.

Broccoli and mushroom quiche with wholegrain garlic crust

Ashley Madden, St John's, Canada

Gluten-free • Serves 6–8

1 onion, diced

3 garlic cloves, finely chopped

225 g (8 oz) cremini or button
mushrooms, sliced

3 cups chopped broccoli

450 g (1 lb) firm tofu

3 tablespoons nutritional yeast

2 tablespoons tahini

1 tablespoon apple cider vinegar

1 tablespoon umeboshi paste or white
miso paste

1 tablespoon tamari or soy sauce

1 teaspoon ground turmeric

Crust

1 teaspoon psyllium husk

3 tablespoons warm water

2 cups freshly cooked long-grain brown
rice or quinoa, cooled slightly

2 tablespoons unsweetened apple sauce

2 tablespoons nutritional yeast

½ teaspoon garlic powder

½ teaspoon Himalayan salt or sea salt

½ teaspoon freshly ground black pepper

Preheat the oven to 190°C (375°F/gas 5) and line the base of a pie dish with baking paper. This can be done easily by tracing the bottom of the pie dish onto the paper and cutting it out.

To make the crust, combine the psyllium husk and water in a bowl and let sit for 5–10 minutes until gelatinous. Combine all the crust ingredients, including the psyllium/water mixture, and mix well. It will be of a thick consistency. Transfer to the lined pie dish and smooth out using a spatula. Bake for 10 minutes. Allow to cool before adding filling.

Cook the onion in a large, heavy-based frying pan over medium heat until translucent, about 5–7 minutes. Make sure to add a bit of water if the onion begins to stick too much and take on colour. You are just looking to soften the onion at this stage and remove its raw flavour. Stir in the garlic and mushrooms and continue to sauté until the mushrooms have released their juices, 5 minutes.

Add the broccoli and cook for 3 minutes until the broccoli is tender and bright green. (Broccoli is overcooked when it is less vibrant and starts to turn olive green.) Remove the pan from the heat.

Add the tofu, nutritional yeast, tahini, vinegar, umeboshi or miso, tamari or soy sauce and turmeric to a food processor and blend until smooth. You may have to scrape down the side as you go. Add the onion mixture and pulse a few times until well incorporated but still chunky.

Spoon the tofu mixture over the crust, smooth the surface and bake for about 45 minutes until the top just starts to brown and firm up. Cover with foil and let sit for 10–15 minutes before cutting.

NOTE: Psyllium husk is the strongest of all binders in vegan cuisine. If you don't have it on hand, flaxseed meal will do.

Noémie's pie

Gaspar Hoyos, Nancy, France
Serves 4–6

Dough
150 ml (5 fl oz) water
1½ tablespoons extra virgin olive oil
200 g (7 oz) plain (all-purpose) flour
2 pinches of baking soda

Filling
3 tablespoons wholegrain mustard
1 onion, thinly sliced
1 large tomato, thinly sliced
½ romanesco broccoli or ½ head of broccoli, chopped
4 egg whites
½ cup plant-based milk
sea salt and freshly ground black pepper
2 tablespoons dry breadcrumbs
2 tablespoons nutritional yeast

Preheat your oven to 180°C (350°F/gas 4) fan-forced. Grease a pie dish with oil.

Use the Tupperware method for preparing the dough. Put the water, oil, flour and baking soda in a container, cover with a lid and shake vigorously.

Dust the worktop with flour, turn out the dough and knead until evenly mixed. Roll out the dough and place it over the prepared pie dish. Spread the mustard generously over the dough, then layer the vegetables, first the onion, followed by the tomato and then the romanesco or broccoli.

Beat the egg whites with your preferred choice of plant-based milk until it's combined. Season with salt and pepper and spoon over the pie.

Prepare the 'fake gratin' by mixing the breadcrumbs with the nutritional yeast. Sprinkle over the pie and bake for 30–40 minutes until the 'gratin' starts to brown.

Zucchini pie

Shona Daube, Carterton, New Zealand

Serves 8

1 large carrot, coarsely grated
400 g (14 oz) zucchini (courgettes), coarsely grated
1 large onion, finely chopped
150 g (5½ oz) firm tofu
sea salt and freshly ground black pepper
1 heaped teaspoon wholegrain mustard
1 cup plain (all-purpose) flour
1 teaspoon baking powder
3 tablespoons extra virgin olive oil, or less to taste
5 egg whites, whisked to soft peaks
pickle or relish and green salad, to serve

Preheat your oven to 160°C (315°F/gas 2–3). Grease a 23 cm (9 inch) pie dish.

Put the vegetables in a bowl and crumble in the tofu. Add all the other ingredients and stir to mix. Fold in the egg white. Transfer to your greased pie dish and bake for 30–40 minutes.

Serve with a pickle or relish and a salad.

Spiced pumpkin filling

Jack McNulty, Zurich, Switzerland

Makes enough for 100 'ravioli'

300 g (10½ oz) cooked pumpkin (squash) pieces, as dry as possible
⅔ cup almond meal
2 teaspoons five-spice
½ teaspoon cayenne pepper
1 teaspoon sea salt
1 tablespoon agave nectar
about 50 g (1¾ oz) matzo meal

Place the pumpkin in a food processor and blend until smooth. Add the almond meal, spices, salt and agave nectar and pulse to combine. Transfer the mixture to a bowl and add just enough matzo meal (you may need to add a touch more or less) to make the mixture semi-firm. The goal here is to make sure your filling is not too wet to work with. It's best to err on the side of firmness. Once you are happy with the consistency, refrigerate the mixture for 24 hours to allow it to firm up.

TIPS: This is a wonderful spiced pumpkin filling which can be used for filling ravioli or tortellini, as a filling for a pie or for vegetarian empanada-like bite-sized pies.

For a quick and easy alternative to homemade pasta, use gyoza wrappers, which you can buy from Asian stores. Just make sure they are OMS-safe.

The real star in this recipe is the five-spice (purchase in Asian stores), which works so well with the slight sharpness from the cayenne pepper.

If you don't have any matzo meal on hand, just use breadcrumbs.

Finally, you can also use maple syrup in place of the agave nectar.

Potato enchilada

Donna Woodruff, Apex, United States

Serves 4

4 large potatoes, peeled and diced

1 onion, chopped

1–2 garlic cloves, finely chopped

½–¾ cup vegetable stock (homemade—for a recipe, see page 110)

2 jalapeno chillies, deseeded and finely chopped

1 teaspoon chilli powder

freshly ground black pepper

1 cup baby spinach leaves

½ cup corn kernels

1 cup cooked black beans

2½ cups Enchilada Sauce, plus extra to serve (see recipe, page 216)

8 corn tortillas (make sure they are OMS-friendly)

salsa, to serve (optional—for a homemade recipe, see page 231)

Preheat the oven to 180°C (350°F/gas 4). Cook the potato in boiling salted water until almost tender, 5–7 minutes. Drain and set aside.

Place the onion and garlic in 3 tablespoons of stock in a large, non-stick frying pan over medium heat and cook, stirring frequently, until the onion softens slightly. Add the chilli and another 3 tablespoons of stock. Cook for an additional minute.

Add the potato, mix well and continue to cook and stir. Add the remaining stock, the chilli powder and several twists of freshly ground pepper. Cook and stir for another minute.

Add the spinach, corn and black beans and mix well, then cook until heated through. Remove from the heat and set aside.

Place ½ cup of enchilada sauce in the bottom of a lightly oiled baking dish. Take one tortilla at a time and spread a line of about 3 tablespoons of potato mixture down the centre of each one. Roll up and place, seam side down, in the baking dish. Repeat until all the filling and tortillas are used. Pour the remaining sauce over the tortillas, cover with foil and bake for 30 minutes. Serve with extra enchilada sauce on the side or with some fresh salsa (if using).

TIPS: Any type of fresh, firm potato may be used in this recipe.

Bottled minced garlic may be used instead of fresh garlic.

If you do not have jalapeno chillies, use 2 tablespoons of canned, chopped green chillies instead.

BURGERS

Broccoli and chickpea burgers

Ingrid Adelsberger, Los Angeles, United States

Makes 4

1 cup water

⅓ cup couscous

1½ cups broccoli florets

½ cup chopped onion

½ cup chopped spring onions (scallions)

2 teaspoons ground cumin

425 g (15 oz) can chickpeas (garbanzo beans), rinsed and drained

1 tablespoon tahini

½ cup dry breadcrumbs

1 teaspoon extra virgin olive oil

Preheat your oven to 200°C (400°F/gas 6). Line a baking tray with foil.

Combine the water and couscous in a small saucepan and bring to the boil. Remove from the heat and allow the couscous to sit in the pan for 10 minutes, soaking up the water.

Steam the broccoli (or use a microwave) for 5–7 minutes until tender.

Cook the onion and spring onion in a heavy-based frying pan over medium heat until translucent. Make sure to add a bit of water if the onion begins to stick too much and take on colour. You are just looking to soften the onion at this stage and remove its raw flavour. Remove the pan from the heat and stir in the cumin.

Place the couscous, broccoli, onion mixture, chickpeas and tahini in a food processor and process until combined. Transfer to a bowl, stir in the breadcrumbs and olive oil, and shape into four burgers. Place the burgers on the prepared tray and bake for 40 minutes, turning them over halfway through. You'll know they are done when the tops begin to brown.

TIP: Add some pickles, tomato, lettuce and mustard or tomato sauce (ketchup) to complete your burger.

Salmon burgers

Abba Renshaw, Auckland, New Zealand

Serves 4

½ large onion, peeled and sliced
pinch of sea salt
2 tablespoons dijon mustard
2 tablespoons finely chopped ginger
1 garlic clove, finely chopped
2 French shallots, finely chopped
1 large handful of coriander (cilantro) leaves and stems
2 salmon fillets, pin-boned and skin removed
4 OMS-friendly buns
lettuce leaves

Preheat the oven to 180°C (350°F). Line a baking tray with baking paper.

Heat a large pot or pan (preferably stainless steel) over medium heat. The pan will have reached the correct temperature when a few drops of water immediately swirl in the pan like mercury balls. At this point, add the chopped onions and immediately season them with salt to help release their water. Allow the onions to gently stew in their juices until they begin to stick on the pan. Release the onions and their juices by adding 1–2 tablespoons of water and gently scraping the pan with a spatula. Continue with the same process until the onions reach a nice golden colour and their juices become brown. This will take 10–15 minutes, so be patient.

Combine the mustard, ginger, garlic, shallot and coriander in a food processor, blitz and transfer to a bowl.

Mince the salmon fillets in the food processor. Be very careful not to overprocess. You don't want to make a paste, you want it quite chunky.

Mix the minced salmon with the mustard mixture and shape into four patties. Place them on the lined baking tray and bake for 20 minutes, turning after 10 minutes.

Serve on the buns with the lettuce and caramelised onions.

Lentil-mushroom burgers

Rae Jackman, Fife, Scotland

Makes 10–12

1 cup dried green lentils

2¼ cups water

1 teaspoon dried parsley

3 garlic cloves, finely chopped

1¼ cups finely chopped onion
  (I use a food processor for this)

3 tablespoons balsamic vinegar

2 tablespoons dijon mustard

¾ cup finely chopped walnuts
  (I use the food processor again)

2 cups fine fresh breadcrumbs
  (I use gluten-free and the food
  processor again)

½ cup flaxseed meal

1 teaspoon sea salt

½ teaspoon freshly ground black pepper

½ teaspoon sweet paprika

3–4 cups finely chopped mixed
  mushrooms (such as cremini, button
  or portobello)

1½ cups finely chopped kale or English
  spinach

Bring the lentils, water, parsley, 1 garlic clove and ¼ cup of onion to the boil in a saucepan. Reduce the heat and simmer, adding more water if necessary, for 35–40 minutes until the water is absorbed and the lentils are soft. Remove from the heat, add the vinegar and mustard and mash with a potato masher to a thick paste.

Combine the walnuts, breadcrumbs and flaxseed meal in a bowl. Add salt, pepper and paprika and mix well.

Sauté the remaining onion and garlic with the mushrooms and greens in 1 tablespoon of water for 8–10 minutes, then set aside.

In a large bowl, combine the lentils, sautéed vegies and breadcrumb mixture and mix well. Cool in the refrigerator for 15–30 minutes or more.

Preheat the oven to 180°C (350°F/gas 4).

Shape the lentil mixture into patties, place on a greased baking tray and bake for about 10 minutes on each side.

 TIP: This recipe makes a large quantity but the burgers freeze well.

Black bean and beetroot burgers

Ingrid Adelsberger, Los Angeles, United States

Makes 6

3 tablespoons rolled (porridge) oats

3 large beetroot (beets)

½ cup long-grain brown rice

1 onion, finely diced

sea salt

4 garlic cloves, finely chopped

2 tablespoons apple cider vinegar

2 × 440 g (15 oz) cans black beans, drained and rinsed

3 tablespoons pitted prunes, finely chopped

1 tablespoon extra virgin olive oil

2 teaspoons dijon mustard

2 teaspoons smoked paprika, or to taste

1 teaspoon ground cumin

1 teaspoon ground coriander

1 teaspoon dried thyme

freshly ground black pepper

1 egg white

Preheat the oven to 180°C (350°F/gas 4).

Place the rolled oats in a food processor and whiz until a flour forms. Set aside.

Wrap the beetroot in foil and roast until easily pierced with a fork, about 1 hour. Set aside until cool enough to handle, then peel.

Meanwhile, cook the rice as per the manufacturer's instructions, adding a few minutes to cook the rice beyond al dente. You want it a little overcooked (not completely mushy). This will take 35–40 minutes. Drain the rice and set aside to cool.

Heat a large, heavy-based frying pan (preferably stainless steel) over medium heat. The pan has reached the correct temperature when a few drops of water immediately swirl in the pan like mercury balls. At this point, add the onion and immediately season with salt to help release its water. Allow the onion to stew gently in its juices until it begins to stick on the pan. Release the onion and its juices by adding 1–2 tablespoons of water and gently scraping the pan with a spatula. Continue with the same process until the onion reaches a nice golden colour and the juices become brown. This will take 10–15 minutes, so be patient. A dark crust will develop on the bottom of the pan. Add the garlic and cook until it is fragrant, about 30 seconds.

Pour in the vinegar, scrape up the dark crust and continue to simmer until the vinegar has evaporated. Remove from the heat and set aside to cool.

Place the black beans in a food processor, scatter the prunes on top and pulse a few times until mushy (some large pieces will remain and that is good as you want the texture). Transfer to a large bowl.

Coarsely grate the peeled beetroot and place in a strainer set over the sink. Press and squeeze out as much liquid as possible.

Add the grated beetroot, cooked rice and sautéed onion to the beans. Sprinkle on the olive oil, dijon mustard, smoked paprika, cumin, coriander and thyme and mix until combined. Taste and add salt, pepper or any additional spices or flavourings to taste.

Finally, add the oat flour and egg white and mix well. Cover the bowl with plastic wrap and refrigerate for 2 hours or (ideally) overnight. The burger mixture will keep in the refrigerator for up to 3 days.

When ready to bake the burgers, preheat the oven to 180°C (350°F/gas 4). Line a baking tray with baking paper. Wet your hands and shape the mixture into six large patties. Place the burgers on the tray and bake for 15 minutes on each side until firm and a bit brown.

TIP: Serve with OMS-friendly burger buns, pickles, sliced tomatoes and a salad on the side.

If time is tight, you can use ready-to-eat beetroot.

Vegetable protein burgers

Ingrid Adelsberger, Los Angeles, United States

Makes 6–7

½ cup rolled (porridge) oats

1 cup dried green lentils

2½ cups water

½ cup warm water

3 tablespoons flaxseed meal

445 g (15 oz) can black beans, rinsed and drained

1 cup cooked quinoa

2–3 garlic cloves, finely chopped

½ red onion, finely chopped

1 red capsicum (bell pepper), finely chopped

⅓ cup walnuts, chopped

1 tablespoon ground cumin

½ teaspoon cayenne pepper

2 teaspoons sriracha (or other hot chilli sauce)

1 teaspoon sea salt

½ teaspoon freshly ground black pepper

½ teaspoon garlic powder

Place the rolled oats in a food processor and whiz until a flour forms. Set aside.

Simmer the lentils in a saucepan with 2½ cups of water until tender, about 20 minutes. Reduce the heat and simmer for 35–40 minutes, adding more water if necessary, until the water is absorbed and the lentils are soft. Set aside.

To make the flax egg, combine the warm water and flaxseed meal in a bowl and let sit for 10 minutes.

Preheat the oven to 190°C (375°F/gas 5). Line a baking tray with baking paper.

Purée the lentils with the black beans and transfer to a large bowl. Add the quinoa, oat flour, garlic, onion, capsicum, walnuts, flax egg and spices. Taste and adjust the spices to your liking.

To form the patties, wet your hands and grab a handful of the mixture and shape it into a ball, then drop onto the prepared tray and press down lightly with your fingers to flatten. Bake for 15 minutes, then flip each patty carefully with a spatula and bake for another 15 minutes.

NOTE: You can refrigerate the mixture for 1 hour. This isn't necessary, but will make your life a lot easier as you form the patties. Also, these patties are a little on the softer side, so be careful when you flip them and take them out of the oven.

GRAINS,
PASTA
AND
NOODLES

Prawn risotto

Geoff Allix, Devon, United Kingdom

Serves 4

1 onion, chopped
2 garlic cloves, finely chopped
250 g (9 oz) arborio rice (or other risotto rice)
½ glass white wine
2 cups vegetable stock (homemade—for a recipe, see page 110)
200 g (7 oz) baby corn, chopped into chunks
200 g (7 oz) snow peas (mangetout)
250 g (9 oz) raw prawns (shrimp), peeled and deveined
1 tablespoon extra virgin olive oil

Cook the onion in a large, heavy-based saucepan over medium heat until translucent. Make sure to add a bit of water if the onion begins to stick too much and take on colour. You are just looking to soften the onion at this stage and remove its raw flavour.

Add the garlic to the pan and fry for 30 seconds. Add the rice, stir and fry for 1 minute. Pour in the wine and stir. Add enough vegetable stock so that the mixture boils rather than fries and bring to the boil.

Stir in the vegetables and keep stirring and adding the vegetable stock to prevent the rice drying out for about 15 minutes. Test the rice to make sure it is nearly cooked. It will be firm and powdery when undercooked. When it is nearly ready, add the prawns and stir until they are cooked. Remove from the heat, add the olive oil and serve.

TIP: To ensure the rice cooks evenly while you're adding the broth, use a wide, heavy-based pan.

Chewy Indonesian rice

Clare Paton, Napier, New Zealand

Gluten-free • Serves 4

1 cup short- or long-grain brown rice
½ cup brown lentils
2 cups boiling water
1 spring onion (scallion), finely chopped
1 red capsicum (bell pepper), finely chopped
1 green capsicum (bell pepper), finely chopped
¼ cup currants
¼ cup crushed almonds
½ teaspoon crushed small dried red chillies or a pinch of chilli flakes
½ teaspoon sea salt
1 teaspoon curry powder
2 tablespoons date syrup or honey

Lemon dressing
3 tablespoons extra virgin olive oil
1 garlic clove, finely chopped
½ teaspoon ground cumin
½ teaspoon sea salt (optional)
2 tablespoons lemon juice

Combine the rice and lentils in a saucepan, add the boiling water, cover with the lid and cook over low heat for around 35 minutes, or until cooked and sticky.

Place the lemon dressing ingredients in a blender and blend (or shake in a jar with a lid).

Combine all the ingredients in a big bowl and serve.

TIP: Replace the almonds with chestnuts if they are in season.

Balkan rice

Beate Zielke, Berlin, Germany

Gluten-free • Serves 4

3 red capsicums (bell peppers), very
  finely chopped
6 onions, very finely chopped
4–6 garlic cloves, very finely chopped
235 g (8½ oz) tomato passata
2 cups long-grain brown or basmati rice
4 cups water

3 teaspoons sea salt
2 teaspoons ground turmeric
pinch of freshly ground black pepper
  (only a small pinch to enhance the
  bioavailability of the turmeric)
1 teaspoon hot paprika
1 tablespoon sweet paprika

Preheat the oven to 140°C (275°C/gas 1).

Put the capsicum, onion and garlic in a large flameproof casserole dish. Stir in the passata, rice, water, salt and spices and bring to the boil. Simmer for 1–3 minutes or so.

Put the lid on the dish and transfer to the oven for 1 hour, stirring halfway through, as the vegetables will have formed a layer on top and the rice a layer on the bottom—you want to have a nice, even mix in which the vegetables are well dispersed.

TIPS: Stir in 1 tablespoon of extra virgin olive oil before placing the rice in the oven. The oil adds to the taste of the dish and may enhance the bioavailability of the liposoluble provitamin A of the capsicum. Or you can add flaxseed oil once the rice is on your plate.

I have also cooked this recipe in a large saucepan on the stovetop instead of in the oven (it needed more attention and stirring in order to prevent sticking and burning).

Ingrid's favourite macro plate

Ingrid Adelsberger, Los Angeles, United States

Gluten-free • Serves 2

1 cup cooked long-grain brown rice
1 cup cooked black beans
1 cup chopped pumpkin (squash)
1 cup chopped broccoli
2 cups chopped kale
1 carrot, chopped into large chunks
3 tablespoons dried hijiki seaweed
Carrot–ginger Dressing (see recipe, page 226)

Cook the rice as per the packet instructions.

While the rice is cooking, heat up the beans and steam all the vegetables. Prepare the seaweed as per the packet instructions (normally by adding warm water).

Arrange the ingredients on a plate and serve with the Carrot-ginger Dressing.

NOTE: I cook this dish when I need something soothing, as it is a well-balanced meal of legumes, grains and healthy vegetables.

VARIATION: Swap the rice for quinoa, the black beans for any other beans or lentils, the kale for spinach—the variations are endless.

Lentil bolognese

Rae Jackman, Fife, Scotland

Serves 3–4

1 onion, finely chopped

2 carrots, coarsely grated

2 garlic cloves, crushed

115 g (4 oz) dried split red lentils

400 g (14 oz) can chopped tomatoes

2 cups vegetable stock (homemade—for a recipe, see page 110)

2 tablespoons tomato paste

125 g (4½ oz) mushrooms, quartered

¼ teaspoon chilli powder

½ teaspoon ground oregano

large pinch of ground coriander (cilantro)

about ½ glass red wine

sea salt and freshly ground black pepper

500 g (1 lb 2 oz) spaghetti

chopped coriander (cilantro), to serve

Cook the onion, carrot and garlic in a heavy-based frying pan over medium heat until the onion turns translucent. Make sure to add a bit of water if the onion begins to stick too much and take on colour. You are just looking to soften the onion at this stage and remove its raw flavour.

Stir in the lentils, tomatoes, stock, tomato paste, mushrooms (and any other vegetable you want to add) and chilli. Season with the oregano, coriander, red wine, salt and pepper. Increase the heat to medium–high and bring to the boil. Reduce the heat to medium and simmer, partly covered, for 20 minutes until the mixture thickens.

Cook the pasta in a large saucepan of boiling salted water until al dente. Drain, toss with the lentil sauce and serve, topped with the chopped coriander.

TIP: The easiest way to prepare the onion, carrot and garlic is to pulse them in a food processor.

Tarka dal

Kerryn Cunningham, Melbourne, Australia

Serves 4

1 cup spit red lentils (masoor dal), rinsed well
3½ cups water
1 teaspoon sea salt, or to taste
4 French shallots, finely chopped
½ teaspoon black or brown mustard seeds
½ teaspoon cumin seeds
2 small green chillies, chopped (deseeded if you like)
1 teaspoon ground turmeric
1 teaspoon ground cumin
1 tomato, chopped
2 tablespoons chopped coriander (cilantro)

Place the lentils in a saucepan, add the water and bring to the boil. Reduce the heat to medium and skim off the foam. Cook, uncovered, for 10 minutes. Reduce the heat to low, cover and cook, stirring occasionally to ensure that the lentils do not stick to the bottom of the pan as they thicken, for 45 minutes. Stir in the salt then remove from the heat.

Meanwhile, fry the shallot in 1 tablespoon of water in a small saucepan over medium heat.

Add the mustard seeds and cook until they begin to pop, then add the cumin seeds and cook them until fragrant.

Add the chilli and cook, stirring, for 2–3 minutes, then add the turmeric and cumin and cook for 2–3 minutes.

Stir in the tomato and cook for 30 seconds. Fold into the cooked lentils, stir in the coriander and serve immediately.

Cauliflower with pasta

Jill Pack, London, United Kingdom

Serves 4

2 tablespoons extra virgin olive oil

1 head of cauliflower, separated into smallish florets

60 g (2 oz) anchovy fillets, drained and patted dry

5 garlic cloves, crushed (more if you like)

sea salt and freshly ground black pepper

500 g (1 lb 2 oz) pasta (shells if possible)

2 tablespoons chopped flat-leaf (Italian) parsley

¼–½ teaspoon freshly ground black pepper

juice of ½ lemon

Preheat the oven to 180°C (350°F/gas 4) or 160°C (315°F/gas 2–3) fan-forced. Oil a baking dish with a good coating of olive oil (but not so it's swimming with it). Add ½ cup of water to ensure the temperature of the oil doesn't get too high and to help the anchovies dissolve.

Place the cauliflower and anchovies in the prepared dish and mix well. Add the garlic, season and roast for 30–40 minutes until the cauliflower is softened.

Meanwhile, cook the pasta in a large saucepan of boiling salted water until al dente. Drain, mix the pasta with the cauliflower and anchovies and add the chopped parsley and pepper. Finally, squeeze over the lemon juice and serve.

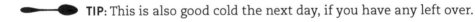 **TIP:** This is also good cold the next day, if you have any left over.

Creamy tofu pasta

Charlotte Ellis, Fareham, United Kingdom

Serves 2–3

175 g (6 oz) pasta, cooked until al dente, drained
40 g (1½ oz) frozen peas, cooked
40 g (1½ oz) corn kernels, cooked
chilli flakes, to sprinkle
sea salt and freshly ground black pepper

Sauce
300 g (10½ oz) silken tofu
4 teaspoons cashew nuts, soaked in water for several hours
1 tablespoon tamari or soy sauce
1 tablespoon extra virgin olive oil
1 tablespoon sweet white miso
1 tablespoon flaxseed oil

Whiz all the sauce ingredients in a food processor or blender until smooth and creamy.

Mix the pasta, peas and corn with the sauce and season with the chilli flakes, salt and pepper to taste.

NOTE: This sauce works well even when cooked with up to 300 g (10½ oz) pasta and lots more peas and corn.

Creamy avocado pasta with prawns

Jenny Nicholson, Fareham, United Kingdom

Gluten-free • Serves 4

250 g (9 oz) wheat/dairy/gluten-free pasta (this is great with spaghetti)
250 g (9 oz) cooked prawns (shrimp), peeled and deveined
50 g (1¾ oz) pine nuts
large pinch of sea salt
freshly ground black pepper

Sauce
2 avocados
1 handful of basil leaves
juice of 1 lemon
2–3 garlic cloves

Cook the pasta in a large saucepan of boiling salted water until just al dente. Add the prawns to warm them through. Drain.

Meanwhile, put all the sauce ingredients into a food processor and blend until smooth and creamy. Scoop this into a large bowl and mix in the pine nuts.

Transfer the cooked pasta and prawns to the sauce. Mix well, before adding salt and pepper to taste. Serve immediately.

TIP: You may like to serve this pasta topped with basil leaves and chopped cherry tomatoes.

Fettuccine Alfredo

J. James, Amsterdam, The Netherlands

Serves 4

375 g (13 oz) fettuccine
2 potatoes, chopped
½ onion, chopped
1 cup water, reserved from boiling the vegetables
½ cup cashew nuts
3 tablespoons nutritional yeast
1 tablespoon Italian herbs
1 teaspoon lemon juice
½ teaspoon sea salt
1 garlic clove, finely chopped

Cook the fettucine in a large saucepan of boiling salted water until al dente. Drain well.

Cook the potato and onion in boiling water for 10 minutes. Drain, but reserve 1 cup of the water.

Put the water in a blender. Add the cashews and nutritional yeast, blend, add the vegies, Italian herbs, lemon juice, salt and garlic and blend.

Place the fettuccine in a bowl, add the alfredo sauce and gently toss to combine.

NOTE: You could also add a chopped boiled tomato (without skin) or vegetables such as broccoli, black olives, grilled (broiled) red capsicum (bell pepper), grilled (broiled) eggplant (aubergine) or zucchini (courgette).

Pasta puttanesca with tuna

Wendy Wood, Murchison, New Zealand

Serves 4

400 g (14 oz) farfalle or penne pasta (something with ridges or holes)
4 garlic cloves, chopped
1 bunch of flat-leaf (Italian) parsley, chopped
16 pitted kalamata olives, roughly chopped
2 tablespoons capers, roughly chopped
10 sun-dried tomatoes, roughly chopped (if in oil, rinse under warm water first)
2 pinches of chilli flakes, or to taste
185 g (6½ oz) can tuna in spring water, drained
sea salt and freshly ground black pepper
glug of flaxseed oil

Cook the pasta in boiling salted water until it is al dente. Drain, reserving approximately 150 ml (5 fl oz) of the cooking water.

Sizzle the garlic in a little of the cooking water, stir in the parsley and add the pasta. Lightly toss through the olives, capers, sun-dried tomatoes and chilli flakes. Flake through the tuna and loosen to taste with the remaining cooking water. Season well with salt and pepper and stir through the flaxseed oil.

Spaghetti with tofu polpette

Ingrid Adelsberger, Los Angeles, United States

Serves 2

1 large onion, peeled

3 garlic cloves, peeled

2–3 sun-dried tomatoes (not in oil)

1 bunch of basil, leaves picked

1 rosemary sprig, leaves picked

175 g (6 oz) firm tofu, crumbled

1 tablespoon dried oregano

1 tablespoon chilli flakes

1 teaspoon nutritional yeast,
  plus extra to serve

1 egg white

3 tablespoons dry breadcrumbs

225 g (8 oz) wholemeal (whole-wheat)
  spaghetti

flaxseed or extra virgin olive oil, to
  drizzle

Sauce

3 tablespoons cherry tomatoes, chopped

½ onion, finely chopped

2 garlic cloves, finely chopped

1 cup tomato passata

2 tablespoons tomato paste

sea salt and freshly ground black
  pepper

Preheat the oven to 180°C (350°F/gas 4). Line a baking tray with baking paper.

Place the onion, garlic, sun-dried tomatoes, most of the basil and rosemary (keep a bit for the tomato sauce) in a food processor and process to a paste. Transfer to a bowl and add the tofu, oregano, chilli flakes, nutritional yeast, egg white and breadcrumbs and mix well. Shape the mixture into small polpette (small meatball-like shapes). Place the balls on a baking tray and bake for 25 minutes. Gently turn the balls and bake for another 25 minutes until golden brown on all sides.

For the sauce, combine the cherry tomatoes, onion, garlic, tomato passata, tomato paste and reserved rosemary in a saucepan and simmer, stirring occasionally, for about 10 minutes. Stir in the reserved basil and season to taste.

Meanwhile, cook the pasta in boiling salted water until al dente. Drain, place on serving plates, add the balls and top with the sauce. Sprinkle on some extra nutritional yeast and drizzle with the desired oil.

NOTE: The balls keep well for 1–2 days in the fridge.

Smoked salmon, broccoli and lemon pasta

Lucie Williams, Paraparaumu, New Zealand

Serves 1

2 handfuls of pasta (such as penne)
½ small head of broccoli, separated into florets
50 g (1¾ oz) smoked salmon, cut into small pieces
¼ preserved lemon, finely diced, or the juice of ½ lemon
sea salt and freshly ground black pepper

Cook the pasta in a large saucepan of boiling salted water and, 5 minutes before the end of the cooking time, add the broccoli. When the pasta is al dente and the broccoli is tender, drain well and return to the pan.

Add the remaining ingredients, stir well and season. Bon appétit!

TIP: Make sure you add the lemon juice just before serving—if you add it too early, the broccoli will turn from an appetising green to greyish.

Pad Thai

Geoff Allix, Devon, United Kingdom

Serves 4

100 g (3½ oz) tamarind slab
200 g (7 oz) rice noodles
3 garlic cloves, chopped
100 g (3½ oz) spring onions (scallions), chopped
3 egg whites, lightly whisked
300 g (10½ oz) firm tofu, chopped
500 g (1 lb 2 oz) bean sprouts
¾ cup snipped chives
⅓ cup chopped almonds
200 g (7 oz) cooked small prawns, peeled (optional)
1 tablespoon tamari or soy sauce
1 tablespoon fish sauce (optional)
1 lemon, cut into wedges

Soak the tamarind in warm water for 30 minutes, then press through a sieve to form a paste.

Soak the rice noodles in water according to the instructions on the packet, then drain.

Dry-fry the garlic and spring onion for 1 minute in a wok. Add the egg whites and cook until just set. Add the tofu, rice noodles and tamarind paste and stir to combine. Add half the bean sprouts, chives and almonds, and the prawns (if using), and cook for 5 minutes. Drizzle on the tamari or soy sauce and fish sauce (if using). Serve with the remaining bean sprouts, chives and almonds and the lemon wedges.

NOTE: You can use tamarind paste instead of a tamarind slab. If you are not used to cooking with fish sauce, either omit it, or just use a little to start with. It is very salty.

Vietnamese stir-fry

Dat Nguyen, New York, United States

Serves 2–3

200 g (7 oz) glass noodles

6 raw prawns (shrimp), peeled and
  deveined

freshly ground black pepper

3 tablespoons fish sauce, or to taste

½ cup vegetable stock (homemade—for
  a recipe, see page 110)

2 garlic cloves, finely chopped

2.5 cm (1 inch) piece of ginger, cut into
  strips

1 carrot, shredded

½ onion, chopped

20 g (¾ oz) dried wood-ear mushrooms,
  soaked in hot water until soft (about
  15 minutes) and finely chopped (you
  can also use other types of mushroom,
  such as portobello or patty straw)

heaped ⅓ cup bean sprouts

1 handful of baby spinach leaves
  (optional)

2–3 celery stalks, cut into thin 7.5 cm
  (3 inch) strips

175–225 g (6–8 oz) tofu, diced

chopped coriander (cilantro), to serve

sriracha (or other hot chilli sauce),
  to serve

Soak the glass noodles in water for 15 minutes. Drain.

Combine the prawns, pepper, 2 teaspoons of fish sauce and the vegetable stock in a bowl, set aside for 15 minutes.

In a wok or large frying pan over medium heat, sauté the garlic and ginger with 1 tablespoon of water until fragrant.

Add the carrot, onion and mushrooms for 1 minute.

Stir in the bean sprouts, spinach (if using), celery and tofu and cook for another minute.

Add the prawn mixture and make some room in the centre of the wok or pan. Toss in the drained glass noodles and gently stir over medium–high heat until the prawns are cooked and the noodles are translucent (this should happen pretty quickly).

Serve with some pepper, coriander and sriracha on top.

ONE-POT
MEALS

Ghanaian fish stew

Jill Pack, London, United Kingdom

Serves 4

1 onion, chopped
½ teaspoon chilli flakes
400 g (14 oz) can chopped tomatoes
3–4 tablespoons almond butter
250 g (9 oz) firm white fish fillets (even coley will be fine), skin removed, chopped
  into large bite-sized pieces
steamed brown rice and steamed broccoli, to serve

Cook the onion in a large, heavy-based frying pan over medium heat until translucent. Make sure to add a bit of water if the onion begins to stick too much and take on colour. You are just looking to soften the onion at this stage and remove its raw flavour. Add the chilli flakes and tomatoes and cook for 10 minutes.

Ladle 2–3 tablespoons of the tomato sauce into a small bowl and gradually mix in the almond butter to create a smooth sauce, making sure it is not too thick and dry—if it is, just add some more tomato sauce. Pour the contents of the pan into the tomato sauce and mix well—taste and add more almond butter, in the same way as before, if the flavour is a bit bland and not particularly nutty.

Add the fish to the sauce and cook for 10–15 minutes—the fish will break up, but this is fine. Serve with brown rice and steamed broccoli.

NOTE: Any leftovers are good on toast the next day. This recipe is adapted from a meal a Ghanaian friend of mine cooked for me when I was at university in the mid-1970s—she made it with chicken, but I prefer it with fish.

Moroccan-style fish stew

Abba Renshaw, Auckland, New Zealand

Serves 2–3

1 onion, sliced
1 garlic clove, finely chopped
2 teaspoons finely chopped ginger
1 teaspoon ground cumin
1 teaspoon ground turmeric
1 teaspoon ground cinnamon
pinch of cayenne pepper
400 g (14 oz) can crushed tomatoes
400 g (14 oz) can chickpeas (garbanzo beans), rinsed
500 g (1 lb 2 oz) white fish fillets, skin removed and chopped into bite-sized pieces
2 teaspoons honey
120 g (4¼ oz) baby spinach leaves
sea salt and freshly ground black pepper
1 tablespoon sliced almonds
finely chopped coriander (cilantro), to serve
couscous, to serve

Cook the onion in a large, heavy-based frying pan over medium heat until translucent. Make sure to add a bit of water if the onion begins to stick too much and take on colour. You are just looking to soften the onion at this stage and remove its raw flavour. Add the garlic, ginger and spices and cook until fragrant, about 2 minutes.

Add the tomatoes, chickpeas and fish and simmer until the fish is just cooked through. Stir in the honey and spinach. Season, top with the almonds and coriander and serve with steamed couscous.

Butternut pumpkin and white fish curry

Jane-Marie Harrison, Beech Cottage, United Kingdom

Serves 4–6

50–100 ml (1¾–3½ fl oz) water
4 cardamom pods
6 black peppercorns
1 cinnamon stick
5 curry leaves (fresh, if possible)
1 bay leaf (fresh, if possible)
1 onion, finely chopped
3–4 garlic cloves (according to taste), finely grated
3 cm (1¼ inch) piece of ginger, finely grated
1–2 small green or red chillies (see note on page 193)
1 teaspoon garam masala
1 teaspoon ground turmeric
½ teaspoon mixed spice
sea salt
2 tomatoes, finely chopped (or use the equivalent amount of canned
    chopped tomatoes)
1 cup almond milk, rice milk or water
500 g (1 lb 2 oz) butternut pumpkin (squash), cut into 2 cm (¾ inch) cubes
400 g (14 oz) any firm white fish fillets, skin removed and chopped into 2 cm
    (¾ inch) cubes
heaped ⅓ cup almond meal
steamed short-grain brown rice and salad, to serve

Put the water, cardamom, peppercorns and cinnamon in a saucepan, bring to
the boil over medium–high heat, cover the pan and simmer for 2 minutes. Do
not allow to boil dry.

Add the curry leaves and bay leaf and cook for another minute. Add the
onion and a little more water, if needed, and cook for 5 minutes until the onion
is very soft.

Add the garlic, ginger, chilli, dried spices, salt and tomato. Stir well and cook
for a further 3 minutes, adding a little more water, if needed.

Add 200 ml (7 fl oz) of the milk or water, cover and simmer gently. Once the sauce has started to boil, reduce the heat to low and cover for 10 minutes. Stir in the pumpkin, then add the fish a few minutes later. Cook for 15 minutes until tender.

Add the almond meal to the pan, stir well, cover again and cook for a further 5 minutes, stirring often to prevent sticking. If your mixture seems too wet, remove the lid and simmer until thickened. If too thick, add extra water. Serve with rice and a side salad. Delicious!

TIP: You can cheat and use a good curry powder but I recommend you give the full version a try. It is well worth it.

NOTE: If you like your curry spicy, slice the chillies and add with the seeds. Less fiery, add chillies, halved lengthways, discard the seeds. Less spicy, add whole chillies that have been pierced four or five times with a sharp knife. Mild, add whole chillies.

Warm bok choy, prawn and lentil salad

Rae Jackman, Fife, Scotland

Serves 4

200 g (7 oz) large raw king prawns (shrimp)
1 small red chilli, deseeded and finely chopped
¾ cup finely chopped coriander (cilantro), plus extra to serve
zest and juice of 1 lime
2 tablespoons light soy sauce
1 tablespoon honey
2 × 400 g (14 oz) cans green lentils, drained and rinsed
1 avocado, sliced
200 g (7 oz) radishes, trimmed and thinly sliced
½ cup water
400 g (14 oz) bok choy (pak choy), ends trimmed
1 lime, cut into quarters, to serve

Place the prawns, half the chilli, coriander and lime juice and the lime zest in a bowl. Stir and leave to marinate for 10 minutes.

In a separate bowl, mix together the soy sauce, the remaining chilli, coriander and lime juice, and the honey. Stir in the lentils, avocado and radish.

Heat the water in a saucepan, add the bok choy and cook until just wilted, a few minutes (or you can steam them). Add the prawns and marinade and heat through.

Divide the lentil salad between four serving bowls and top with the prawns and bok choy. Sprinkle on a little extra coriander and serve with the lime wedges.

Madras potato curry

Rae Jackman, Fife, Scotland

Serves 4

680 g (1 lb 8 oz) potatoes, cut into 1 cm (½ inch) cubes
250 g (9 oz) cauliflower florets
1 large onion, sliced
2 garlic cloves, crushed
1 tablespoon curry powder
½ tablespoon ground ginger
100 g (3½ oz) dried red lentils
400 g (14 oz) can chopped tomatoes
1 cup vegetable stock (homemade—for a recipe, see page 110)
2 tablespoons malt vinegar
1 tablespoon mango chutney
sea salt and freshly ground black pepper
chopped flat-leaf (Italian) parsley, to garnish

Warm a little water in a large, deep frying pan over medium heat, then stir in the potato, cauliflower, onion and garlic and cook gently until softened, about 5 minutes.

Stir in the curry powder and ginger and cook for 3 minutes until fragrant.

Add the lentils, tomatoes, vegetable stock, vinegar and chutney and stir to combine. Season with salt and pepper, then cover and simmer, stirring occasionally, until the lentils are tender, 20–25 minutes. Garnish with the parsley.

Lecsó (Hungarian vegetable stew)

Judit Gulyás, Debrecen, Hungary

Gluten-free • Serves 3–4

2 onions, chopped
3 garlic cloves, finely chopped
3–4 yellow capsicums (bell peppers), deseeded and sliced
3–4 tomatoes, sliced
sea salt and freshly ground black pepper
homemade wholegrain bread, to serve

Cook the onion in a heavy-based frying pan over medium heat until translucent. Make sure to add a bit of water if the onion begins to stick too much and take on colour. You are just looking to soften the onion at this stage and remove its raw flavour. Add the garlic and sauté for another 1–2 minutes.

Add the capsicum and cook, adding more water if necessary, for 3–4 minutes.

Stir in the tomatoes, season the lecsó with salt and pepper and cover the saucepan with a lid. Cook until the vegetables are soft. Serve with wholegrain bread.

TIPS: Add zucchini (courgette) or vegetable marrow or pumpkin (squash) to make the dish even richer.

Serve the lecsó with boiled brown rice or millet.

Lecsó can also be served with steamed white fish.

If you like your dishes spicy, add some chilli to taste.

Chickpea stew with silverbeet (Swiss chard)

George Jelinek, Melbourne, Australia

Serves 4

2 onions, chopped

1 bunch of silverbeet (Swiss chard), stalks sliced into small pieces, leaves shredded

4 garlic cloves, finely chopped

2 tablespoons ground cumin

4 tablespoons tomato paste

4 tablespoons Middle Eastern spices (see the tip below)

2–4 tablespoons harissa paste, depending on taste

24 cherry tomatoes, halved

2 × 400 g (14 oz) cans chickpeas (garbanzo beans), rinsed and drained

4 tablespoons apple cider vinegar

500 g (1 lb 2 oz) couscous

4 tablespoons flaxseed oil, plus extra to serve

salt and freshly ground black pepper

1 cup soy yoghurt

Sauté the onion in a tagine or deep non-stick frying pan with a little water for 5 minutes over medium heat, stirring frequently. Add the silverbeet stalks and cook for another 5 minutes, adding water as necessary to stop sticking.

Stir in the garlic, cumin, tomato paste, spices, harissa, half the cherry tomatoes, the chickpeas and a little more water to keep everything moist and cook for 3 minutes.

Add the silverbeet leaves, vinegar and a little water, cover and cook over low heat for 3–4 minutes until the silverbeet is wilted.

Meanwhile, prepare the couscous according to the instructions on the packet, usually just by bringing a cup of water for each cup of couscous to the boil in a saucepan, turning off the heat, adding the couscous and leaving, covered, for 3–5 minutes. Prior to serving, fluff with a fork and stir through the flaxseed oil.

Season the tagine, top with the remaining cherry tomatoes, the yoghurt plus a drizzle of flaxseed oil and serve with the couscous.

TIP: You can buy a ready-made Middle Eastern spice mix, or make your own: there are lots of recipes on the internet for dry-roasting spices such as paprika, cumin, turmeric, oregano or thyme, black pepper and ginger.

Autumn glory

Kath, Mildura, Australia

Serves 4–6

1 kg (2 lb 4 oz) pumpkin (squash), cut into large dice
2 onions, sliced
2.5 cm (1 inch) piece of ginger, grated or finely chopped
2 zucchini (courgettes), diced
115 g (4 oz) mushrooms, sliced
400 g (14 oz) can diced tomatoes
1½ cups pasta shells
450 ml (16 fl oz) vegetable stock (homemade—for a recipe, see page 110)
1 handful of basil
sea salt and freshly ground black pepper
2 tablespoons extra virgin olive oil (optional)

Place the pumpkin, onion and ginger in a large saucepan over medium heat and fry, stirring occasionally, in ¼ cup of water for 10 minutes.

Add the zucchini and mushrooms and cook for 10 minutes.

Stir in the tomatoes, pasta, vegetable stock and basil and bring to the boil. Cover, reduce the heat to low and simmer for 10 minutes until the pasta is al dente and the pumpkin is tender. Season to taste and drizzle with olive oil (if using).

Moroccan-style vegetable stew

Phil Hassell, Point Lonsdale, Australia

Serves 4

300 g (10½ oz) dried chickpeas (garbanzo beans), soaked overnight in water, rinsed and cooked until soft

400 g (14 oz) can brown lentils, rinsed and drained

2 small onions, cut into wedges

2 garlic cloves, crushed

2 teaspoons ground coriander

1 teaspoon each ground ginger, sweet paprika, ground turmeric

½ teaspoon ground cinnamon

3 cups vegetable stock (homemade—for a recipe, see page 110)

2 tablespoons tomato paste

⅔ cup dried apricots

400 g (14 oz) new potatoes, peeled and diced

1 large zucchini (courgette), thickly sliced

¼ cabbage, thickly sliced

couscous, to serve

Combine the chickpeas, lentils, onion, garlic, spices, stock, tomato paste, dried apricots and potatoes in a large saucepan and bring to the boil, reduce the heat, cover and simmer, stirring occasionally, for 10 minutes.

Add the vegetables and cook, uncovered, for 20 minutes until the vegetables are tender. Serve the vegetable curry on couscous.

 Consider investing in an electric rice cooker. Most have a timer and programs, such as the 'keep warm' function, that allow you to cook mixed rice dishes. This is a great way to cook interesting meals without using oil. We often add frozen vegetables and seafood then, before serving, add a squeeze of lemon, some condiments, a dash of soy sauce and flaxseed oil.

Carl Herring, Setagaya-ku, Hanegi, Japan

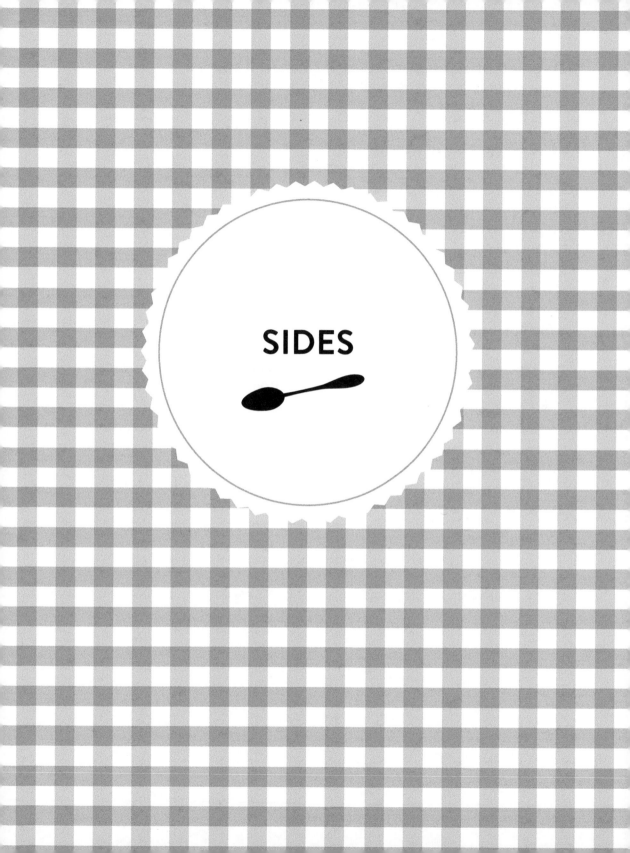

SIDES

Steamed brussels sprouts and tahini dill sauce

Ashley Madden, St John's, Canada

Gluten-free • Serves 2

2 cups trimmed brussels sprouts

Sauce
3 tablespoons tahini
3 tablespoons water
juice of ½ lemon
1 teaspoon dried dill
¼ teaspoon garlic powder
¼ teaspoon Himalayan salt or sea salt, plus extra to serve
⅛ teaspoon freshly ground black pepper, plus extra to serve

To make the sauce, combine all the ingredients in a small blender and blend until smooth. Alternatively, whisk all the ingredients in a bowl. Set aside.

Put a steamer basket over a saucepan of simmering water (make sure the water doesn't rise above the steamer basket), add the brussels sprouts, cover and steam for 5–7 minutes. Do *not* overcook. The brussels sprouts are done when they are bright green and you can just pierce them with a fork.

In a large bowl, add the cooked brussels sprouts and drizzle on as much sauce as you desire. I usually add 3–4 tablespoons. Toss and season with pepper and salt.

Layered potatoes

Jane-Marie Harrison, Beech Cottage, United Kingdom

Serves 6–8 (or 4 as a main)

½ cup extra virgin olive oil
1 garlic clove, cut in half
2 cups rice milk
a few thyme sprigs
1 bay leaf
1.5 kg (3 lb 5 oz) potatoes, thinly sliced
3 onions, thinly sliced
ground allspice
freshly ground black pepper

Preheat the oven to 180°C (350°F/gas 4).

Using a small amount of olive oil, grease a flameproof casserole dish. Rub the cut surface of the garlic over the inside of the dish. The rest of the garlic can be put into the dish to add flavour.

Add the thyme sprigs and the bay leaf to the rice milk and heat it until the milk reaches 60°C (140°F). Remove from the heat, cover and set aside for about 15 minutes, then pour it through a sieve and discard the herbs.

Arrange a layer of potato in the bottom of the dish, then add a layer of onion and the remaining garlic. Sprinkle on a generous pinch of allspice, grind over some pepper and drizzle over some olive oil. Repeat this process until all the potato and onion is used, finishing with a layer of potato. Pour over the herb-infused rice milk and drizzle any remaining olive oil over the top.

Place the casserole over medium heat for about 4 minutes before transferring to the oven. (If you are not using a flameproof dish, either heat the milk before adding it to the vegetables or add 10 minutes to the cooking time.) Bake for 1 hour until the potatoes are cooked and the top is golden brown.

TIP: This recipe also works well with root vegetables or a mixture of potatoes, onions and root vegetables.

Roasted fennel with olives and garlic

Ingrid Adelsberger, Los Angeles, United States

Serves 6

4 small fennel bulbs, trimmed, each cut into 8 wedges with core attached
16 cherry tomatoes halved
2 tablespoons extra virgin olive oil
6 large garlic cloves, coarsely crushed
1 tablespoon chopped thyme
⅛ teaspoon crushed dried red chilli flakes
sea salt and freshly ground black pepper
3 tablespoons halved pitted kalamata olives

Preheat the oven to 200°C (400°F/gas 6). Line a baking tray with baking paper.

Combine the fennel, tomato, olive oil, garlic, thyme and chilli in a large bowl and toss.

Spread the fennel and tomato on the prepared tray and sprinkle with salt and pepper. Roast for 15 minutes, turning the wedges over with tongs. Continue to roast, turning one more time, until almost tender, about 15 minutes.

Sprinkle the olives over the fennel and roast until the fennel is tender and begins to brown at the edges, 5–10 minutes. Season with salt and pepper, transfer to a serving bowl and enjoy.

Crispy oven fries

Ingrid Adelsberger, Los Angeles, United States

Serves 4

4–5 potatoes, cut into strips
1 tablespoon extra virgin olive oil
sea salt and freshly ground black pepper
1–2 teaspoons fresh or dried thyme
2 garlic cloves, finely chopped

Preheat the oven to 200°C (400°F/gas 6). Line a baking tray with baking paper.

In a large bowl, toss the potato with the oil, salt and pepper, thyme and garlic. Place on the prepared tray and bake, turning once after 20 minutes, until golden and crisp, about 35–40 minutes.

Honey-mustard glazed green beans

Ingrid Adelsberger, Los Angeles, United States

Serves 4–6

900 g (2 lb) green beans, trimmed
3 tablespoons mustard seeds
⅓ cup honey
⅓ cup rice vinegar
1 garlic clove, finely chopped
1 tablespoon flaxseed oil or extra virgin olive oil

Bring a large saucepan of lightly salted water to the boil. Add the green beans and cook for 5–7 minutes until tender but still crisp. Drain. (Up to this point, the beans can be cooked ahead of time. Rinse them with cold water to stop them cooking, then place them in a covered container and put them in the fridge.)

In a large saucepan, toast the mustard seeds over low heat, stirring to prevent scorching, until they start to pop, about 1 minute.

Add the honey and vinegar and cook until the sauce boils and becomes a syrup. Add the garlic and cook for 1 minute. Toss the green beans in the syrup, then drizzle with the oil.

NOTE: I like the beans more on the raw side, so I boil them for only 5 minutes.

Sugar snap peas with mint

Ingrid Adelsberger, Los Angeles, United States

Serves 4

900 g (2 lb) sugar snap peas, tough strings removed
½ cup loosely packed chopped mint
1 tablespoon extra virgin olive oil
sea salt
½ teaspoon freshly ground black pepper

Steam the sugar snap peas for 4–5 minutes, or until tender but still crisp.
Combine the sugar snap peas, mint, olive oil and salt and pepper; toss well.

Cheesy-baked broccoli

Ingrid Adelsberger, Los Angeles, United States

Serves 4

6 cups bite-sized broccoli florets and thinly sliced stalks

2–3 tablespoons tamari or soy sauce

1 teaspoon maple syrup

1–2 tablespoons extra virgin olive oil

½ cup nutritional yeast

½ teaspoon freshly ground black pepper

¼ teaspoon chilli flakes

Preheat the oven to 200°C/400°F/gas 6.

Mix all the ingredients in a large bowl, then spread in a single layer on a baking tray. Bake for 20–30 minutes until tender and caramelised. (The cooking time will depend on how large your broccoli florets are.)

Roasted cauliflower curry

Anonymous

Serves 4

3 tablespoons extra virgin olive oil

2 teaspoons curry powder

2 teaspoons honey (or less)

1 teaspoon lemon juice

½ teaspoon sea salt (omit if you feel this is inflammation responsive to your MS)

¼ teaspoon freshly ground black pepper

4 cups cauliflower florets

2 tablespoons slivered almonds

Preheat the oven to 200°C (400°F/gas 6).

Mix the olive oil, curry powder, honey, lemon juice and salt and pepper in a small bowl.

Place the cauliflower florets in a 33 × 23 cm (13 × 9 inch) baking dish, pour the oil mixture over the top and toss gently. Cover with foil and bake for 15 minutes. Remove from the oven and stir in the almonds. Return, uncovered, to the oven and bake for an additional 10–15 minutes until the cauliflower is browned and the almonds are toasted. Transfer the cauliflower to a large serving bowl and serve.

TIP: Try sprinkling pine nuts, coriander (cilantro) and mint over the cauliflower before serving.

Lemon asparagus

Angela Win, Auckland, New Zealand
Serves 2–3

juice of 1 large lemon
2 teaspoons extra virgin olive oil
sea salt and freshly ground black pepper
450 g (1 lb) asparagus

In a large bowl, combine the lemon juice, olive oil, salt and pepper. Set aside.

Remove the woody ends from the asparagus by snapping each spear and allowing it to break naturally. Simmer the asparagus in boiling salted water for 2–3 minutes, depending on thickness. Drain and add to the lemon juice mixture while hot. Coat well, adjust seasoning and serve immediately.

Creamed spinach

Ingrid Adelsberger, Los Angeles, United States

Serves 6

550 g (1 lb 4 oz) baby spinach leaves
2 French shallots, thinly sliced
3 tablespoons plain (all-purpose) flour
1–1½ cups almond milk
½ cup nutritional yeast
sea salt and freshly ground black pepper
2 tablespoons finely chopped almonds
3 tablespoons dry breadcrumbs

Preheat the oven to 180°C (350°F/gas 4).

In a large saucepan, heat 2.5 cm (1 inch) of water. Add the spinach by the handful and allow each handful to wilt before adding more. When all the spinach is wilted, drain and press out as much water as possible.

Place the shallots in a large saucepan, add a few spoonfuls of water (you can use the excess water from the spinach) and sauté over medium heat until softened. Stir in the flour and cook for 1 minute (this is really doable without any oil—just keep stirring and adding more water spoon by spoon, if needed, to make a creamy mixture).

Pour in the almond milk and simmer, whisking occasionally, until very thick, 5 minutes.

Stir in the nutritional yeast and spinach and season with salt and pepper. Spoon into a baking dish, sprinkle on the almonds and breadcrumbs (you may also just choose one or the other) and bake for 15–20 minutes until golden.

Rice with kale

Ingrid Adelsberger, Los Angeles, United States

Serves 4

1 onion, chopped

1–2 small red chillies, chopped

½ bunch of kale, thick stems removed, leaves chopped (about 3 cups)

sea salt and freshly ground black pepper

1 cup long-grain brown rice

1¾ cups vegetable stock (homemade—for a recipe, see page 110)

Heat a large, heavy-based saucepan over medium heat. Add ¼ cup of water and then the onion, chilli and kale, season with salt and pepper and cook, tossing occasionally, until tender, 8–10 minutes.

Add the rice and vegetable stock, reduce the heat to low and simmer, covered, until the rice is tender, 30–35 minutes.

SAUCES, DRESSINGS AND TOPPINGS

Vegan béchamel sauce

Jack McNulty, Zurich, Switzerland

Makes about 2 cups

2 cups plant-based milk
1½ tablespoons extra virgin olive oil
3 heaped tablespoons plain (all-purpose) flour
2 teaspoons rice flour
sea salt
freshly grated nutmeg

Heat the milk in a saucepan over medium–low heat until just on the verge of boiling.

While heating the milk, put the oil in a heavy-based saucepan over low heat. Mix the two flours together and whisk them into the oil. Continue to whisk the mixture for a couple of minutes, then slowly add the warmed milk, while continuing to whisk. Season with salt and the nutmeg and cook over low heat for 30 minutes until the sauce is smooth and relatively thick. Remove from the heat and strain into a clean container.

Use right away, or place some plastic wrap on the surface of the sauce, to prevent a skin from forming, and cool to room temperature before refrigerating.

NOTE: When you heat up the oil, heat it on very low. The oil just needs to be warm, not hot.

Barbecue sauce

Jack McNulty, Zurich, Switzerland

Makes about 2 cups

1 red onion, diced

4 garlic cloves, finely chopped

1 tablespoon ground cumin

1 tablespoon chilli powder

1½ tablespoons onion powder

100 ml (3½ fl oz) vegetable stock (homemade—for a recipe, see page 110)

2 cups diced tomatoes

½ cup tomato paste

½ cup date paste

1½ tablespoons wholegrain mustard

3 tablespoons apple cider vinegar

½ teaspoon liquid smoke (optional)

½ teaspoon freshly ground black pepper

2 tablespoons hot sauce of choice (optional)

½ teaspoon sea salt (optional)

To start the sauce, cook the onion in a heavy-based frying pan over medium heat until translucent. Make sure to add a bit of water if the onion begins to stick too much and take on colour. You are just looking to soften the onion at this stage and remove its raw flavour.

Add the garlic, cumin, chilli powder and onion powder and stir until the spices are lightly toasted. Next, add the vegetable stock and tomatoes. Bring to a simmer and cook for 4–5 minutes.

To finish the sauce, add the tomato paste, date paste, mustard, vinegar, liquid smoke (if using) and pepper. Stir very well and reduce the heat to low. Cover and cook gently for 7–8 minutes. Add the hot sauce (if using) and, with a food processor or hand-held blender, blend until smooth. Season with salt to taste (if using).

NOTE: If not serving immediately, cool and store the barbecue sauce in a sealed container in the refrigerator. This sauce is great to brush on grilled (broiled) vegetables or plant proteins such as tofu, tempeh, eggplant (aubergine), capsicum (bell pepper), onion and tomatoes on the barbecue (see the Tempeh Kebabs with Barbecue Sauce recipe on page 114)—or simply bake tofu or tempeh in it.

Enchilada sauce

Jack McNulty, Zurich, Switzerland

Makes about 4 cups

2 tablespoons plain (all-purpose) flour

1 tablespoon cacao powder

2 tablespoons chilli powder

½ teaspoon cayenne pepper

2 teaspoons dried oregano

2 teaspoons ground cumin

1 teaspoon onion powder

3 cups vegetable stock (homemade—for a recipe, see page 110)

400 ml (14 fl oz) tomato purée

sea salt and freshly ground black pepper

Whisk together the flour, cacao powder and spices in a saucepan. Add about 100 ml (3½ fl oz) of vegetable stock and 100 ml (3½ fl oz) of tomato purée and cook gently over low heat, while slowly whisking. Continue to slowly whisk in the remaining tomato purée and vegetable stock and bring to a gentle boil. Cook for a few minutes until the sauce thickens slightly. When done, it will look like a thin tomato soup. Remove from the heat and season.

Place the sauce in a blender and pulse a few times to create a smoother texture.

Sicilian-style tomato sauce

Jack McNulty, Zurich, Switzerland

Serves 4

2 tablespoons water
2 garlic cloves, peeled
2 fresh bay leaves
400 g (14 oz) Sicilian tomatoes (or very flavourful tomatoes), puréed
4 tablespoons tomato paste
2½ tablespoons white wine
cayenne pepper and sweet paprika, to taste
sea salt and freshly ground black pepper
1 cinnamon stick
1 teaspoon ground cinnamon
extra virgin olive oil, to finish
2 tablespoons chopped flat-leaf (Italian) parsley

Heat a frying pan over medium heat. Add the water, then add the garlic, bay leaves and tomato purée and stir well.

Mix the tomato paste with the white wine, then add to the tomato mixture. Add the cayenne pepper, paprika, salt and pepper and cook for no longer than 10 minutes.

Add the cinnamon stick and ground cinnamon, remove the pan from the heat and stir well. Adjust the seasoning, then add a bit of olive oil. Cover and cool. Reheat over gentle heat, then add the parsley before serving.

NOTE: Use the freshest possible tomatoes for this sauce and do not cook them for too long so they preserve their fresh flavour.

Vegan gravy

Hester Dekker, Vught, The Netherlands

Serves 3–4

15 g (½ oz) dried porcini (cep) mushrooms
1 cup hot water
1 onion, finely chopped
1–2 teaspoons dried thyme
dash of extra virgin olive oil
1 tablespoon tomato purée
splash of tamari or soy sauce
freshly ground black pepper

Put the mushrooms in a bowl and add the hot water. Leave to soak for half an hour. Drain, reserving the liquid.

Put the onion, thyme, olive oil and 1–2 tablespoons of water in a heavy-based frying pan over low heat and fry, stirring occasionally, for at least 10 minutes. Keep adding water.

Add the mushrooms and tomato purée and cook for a moment. Add the liquid from the mushrooms and stir well. Cook for a few more minutes until the gravy thickens. Strain into a bowl and add the tamari or soy sauce and pepper.

NOTE: You can chop the mushrooms into little pieces and add them to the gravy or leave them out.

TIP: Double the quantities, pour the gravy into ice-cube trays and freeze. Thaw a cube when needed.

Vegan tzatziki

Ingrid Adelsberger, Los Angeles, United States

Gluten-free • Serves 4

1 cucumber, peeled and grated
400 g (14 oz) firm tofu
1–2 tablespoons soy yoghurt
2 teaspoons lemon juice (freshly squeezed is best)
2 teaspoons dill gherkin (pickle) juice or apple cider vinegar
1–2 garlic cloves, chopped (2 is pretty garlicky)
1 teaspoon onion powder
½ teaspoon freshly ground black pepper
½ bunch of dill, chopped
sea salt

Place the cucumber in some muslin and twist it tight to squeeze out as much liquid as possible. Set aside.

Add all the ingredients except the cucumber to a blender and blend until smooth; you may need to scrape down the side and blitz again to get a smooth, creamy consistency. Pour into a bowl, season with salt and pepper and add the cucumber. Alternatively, add all the ingredients to the blender and make a tzatziki sauce.

 TIP: Tzatziki can be eaten over rice and vegetables or a baked potato.

Silken tofu mayonnaise

Ingrid Adelsberger, Los Angeles, United States

Gluten-free • Makes about 1 cup

115 g (4 oz) silken tofu
2 teaspoons lemon juice (freshly squeezed is best)
2 teaspoons dijon mustard
⅓–½ cup flaxseed oil or extra virgin olive oil, if you prefer the taste
sea salt

Combine the tofu, lemon juice and mustard in a blender or food processor and process until smooth, about 30 seconds.

Transfer the mixture to a clean bowl, then slowly pour in the oil, whisking to create an emulsified mixture (if you process the oil with the other ingredients, the oil will become oxidised rather quickly). Adjust the seasoning, if needed.

NOTE: I think it works absolutely fine with just ⅓ cup of oil; however, if you need a really creamy consistency, adding more oil will achieve that. If you use flaxseed oil, consider this a delicious guilt-free staple that is a great way to get your daily dose of flaxseed oil.

Lemongrass paste

Ingrid Adelsberger, Los Angeles, United States

Makes ½ cup

2 teaspoons extra virgin olive oil

2 large French shallots, finely chopped

1 tablespoon grated ginger

4–5 garlic cloves, finely chopped

1 lemongrass stem, white part only, bruised and cut into 1 cm (½ inch) pieces, or
  1 tablespoon dried lemongrass

½ teaspoon ground turmeric

1 small red chilli, deseeded and thinly sliced, to taste

Place all the ingredients in a blender or food processor and whiz until very smooth, 2–3 minutes. Transfer to a jar, cover with the lid and keep refrigerated for up to 1 week.

NOTE: Water may help with blending the ingredients, so add a tablespoon, if needed.

Ginger miso dressing

Ingrid Adelsberger, Los Angeles, United States

Makes about 1 cup

1 tablespoon finely grated orange zest

½ cup orange juice (freshly squeezed is best)

2 tablespoons miso paste

2 tablespoons finely grated ginger

2 garlic cloves, finely grated

2 tablespoons tamari or soy sauce

½ cup extra virgin olive oil (or a mixture of flaxseed oil and extra virgin olive oil)

1 teaspoon sea salt

Place the orange zest and juice and the rest of the ingredients in a blender. Blend on low, increase the speed to medium and whiz until the dressing is completely emulsified.

NOTE: The dressing will keep for at least a week in the fridge. I use it over steamed vegetables and grains.

Soy yoghurt dressing

Ingrid Adelsberger, Los Angeles, United States

Serves 2

1 garlic clove, finely chopped
½ cup soy yoghurt
1 tablespoon flaxseed oil or extra virgin olive oil
1 teaspoon dijon mustard
1 teaspoon balsamic vinegar
1 teaspoon snipped chives (dried chives work too)
sea salt and freshly ground black pepper

Place the garlic in a small bowl and add the soy yoghurt, oil, mustard, vinegar and chives. Mix well and add salt and pepper to taste.

 Make your sauces, dressings, toppings and spreads in big quantities and freeze them. This will save you a lot of time and also make living on the OMS diet a lot easier.

Hester Dekker, Vught, The Netherlands

Oil-free roasted red capsicum vinaigrette

Ashley Madden, St John's, Canada

Serves 4

1 large red capsicum (bell pepper)
2 roasted garlic cloves, finely chopped
2 tablespoons balsamic vinegar
2 tablespoons apple cider vinegar
1 tablespoon maple syrup
1½ teaspoons thyme or ½ teaspoon dried thyme
½ teaspoon dried oregano
½ teaspoon dried rosemary
¼ teaspoon sea salt
¼ teaspoon freshly ground black pepper

Preheat the oven to 180°C (350°F/gas 4).

Place the capsicum on a baking tray and roast for 40 minutes until charred. Let cool for 5 minutes, then deseed it.

Combine all the ingredients in a blender and blend until smooth.

NOTE: This vinaigrette can be used on salads and steamed vegies or a baked potato.

Flaxseed dijon vinaigrette

Ingrid Adelsberger, Los Angeles, United States

Gluten-free • Serves 4

1 tablespoon dijon mustard
2 tablespoons flaxseed oil
1 tablespoon lemon juice
1 tablespoon water
1 garlic clove, finely chopped
sea salt and freshly ground black pepper

Combine all the ingredients in a small bowl and mix well. Keep in the fridge in an airtight container for 1–2 days.

TIPS: You can add any herbs you have at home. Replace the lemon juice with orange juice.

Carrot-ginger dressing

Ingrid Adelsberger, Los Angeles, United States

Gluten-free • Serves 4

2 large carrots, chopped
2.5 cm (1 inch) piece of ginger, peeled and chopped
1 tablespoon extra virgin olive oil or flaxseed oil
1 teaspoon sesame oil (for flavour)
1 tablespoon umeboshi plum vinegar or rice vinegar
¼–½ cup water
1 garlic clove, chopped

Combine all the ingredients in a food processor or blender and process until smooth. This dressing will keep for 1 week if stored in the fridge.

 TIP: Use this delicious dressing with grains, legumes and vegetables.

Simple honey lemon dressing

Ingrid Adelsberger, Los Angeles, United States

Serves 2

1 teaspoon finely grated lemon zest
2 tablespoons lemon juice
½–1 tablespoon honey (depending on desired sweetness)
½ teaspoon chopped thyme
½ teaspoon oregano
1 tablespoon extra virgin olive oil
1 tablespoon flaxseed oil
sea salt and freshly ground black pepper

In a small bowl, whisk the lemon zest and juice with the honey, thyme and oregano. Whisk in the oils and season with salt and pepper.

Balsamic dressing

Ingrid Adelsberger, Los Angeles, United States

Makes about 1 cup

3 tablespoons flaxseed oil

3 tablespoons extra virgin olive oil

3 tablespoons balsamic vinegar

1 tablespoon maple syrup (optional)

1 tablespoon dijon mustard

1 garlic glove, finely chopped

sea salt and freshly ground black pepper

Combine all the ingredients in a jar and shake well. You can keep this dressing in the fridge for a few days.

Gawler Foundation salad dressing

Sarah Myers, Sonning Common, United Kingdom

Makes 3 cups

2 cups flaxseed oil
1 cup apple cider vinegar
3 garlic cloves, crushed
2 teaspoons dijon mustard
3 tablespoons honey

Mix all the ingredients together in a blender and store in the refrigerator in a glass bottle or jar for up to 1 week. Use on salads, baked fish, pasta, etc.

 I make my own OMS salad dressing and when going out take it with me in a sneaky container. I ask for salad with no dressing and then add mine. I don't think anyone even notices.

Jo, Freshwater, Australia

Almond shaker

Jack McNulty, Zurich, Switzerland

Gluten-free • Makes 1 cup

¾ cup almond meal
3–4 tablespoons nutritional yeast
½ teaspoon onion powder
½ teaspoon garlic powder
½ teaspoon sea salt

Combine all the ingredients and mix well. Store in an airtight container in the fridge for several weeks.

TIPS: Use this delicious plant-based parmesan substitute to sprinkle on top of pasta, pizza, gratins, salads and your favourite vegetable dishes. You can also substitute ground cashew nuts or pine nuts for the almond meal. For a nice variation, try mixing in some herbs. I like to use sage.

Salsa fresca

Jack McNulty, Zurich, Switzerland

Serves 4

The classic Mexican-style salsa is called *Pico de Gallo*, which is typically made with tomatoes, onions, fresh coriander, chilli and lime juice. Interestingly, if you cross the Atlantic and find yourself in Morocco, you will encounter a sauce which is very familiar. It is called chermoula, and typically includes the same ingredients . . . only replacing the lime with lemon and vinegar and adding a touch of cumin. This version is more along the lines of the Moroccan salsa, but it would go nicely with any Mexican or Central American dish.

1 medium-sized onion, peeled and finely chopped

5–6 tomatoes, deseeded and finely chopped

1 bunch fresh coriander, roughly chopped

1 bunch fresh parsley, roughly chopped

1 clove garlic, grated

2 tablespoons sherry wine vinegar

juice of 1 lemon

1 teaspoon sea salt

2 teaspoons sweet paprika

cayenne pepper to taste (usually ¼ teaspoon)

1 teaspoon ground cumin

Combine the onion and tomato in a large glass bowl. Add the fresh herbs, then the garlic. Mix together and leave to stand for 5 minutes.

Combine the vinegar, lemon juice and all of the seasonings. Add this dressing to the tomato mixture and mix well. Adjust the seasoning and serve right away.

Mustard vinaigrette

Ingrid Adelsberger, Los Angeles, United States

Serves 4

2 garlic cloves, minced

juice of 2 lemons

2 teaspoons dijon mustard

4–6 tablespoons extra virgin olive oil (or a blend of extra virgin olive oil and
flaxseed oil)

salt and pepper to taste

To make the vinaigrette, place the ingredients in a bowl and mix well.

BREADS, QUICKBREADS AND PIECRUSTS

Banana ginger apple muffins

Jessica van Esch, County Kerry, Ireland

Makes 12

2 ripe bananas

3 tablespoons extra virgin olive oil

¾ cup soy milk

2 cups wholemeal (whole-wheat) or plain (all-purpose) flour

1 cup sugar (can be less)

1 teaspoon finely grated ginger or ginger paste

1 teaspoon ground cinnamon

1 teaspoon sea salt (or less; I use a small pinch)

2½ teaspoons baking powder

2 apples, 1 grated and 1 diced

1 handful of chopped walnuts (optional)

12 walnut halves, for decorating (optional)

Preheat the oven to 180°C (350°F/gas 4). Grease a muffin tin with a little extra virgin olive oil, or line it with muffin liners.

Place the bananas in a bowl and mash with a fork. Mix in the oil and milk (or do this in a food processor).

In another bowl, combine the flour, sugar, ginger, cinnamon, salt and baking powder.

Combine the two mixtures together, add the grated and diced apple and the chopped walnuts (if using) and mix. Pour the batter into the prepared muffin tin until about three-quarters full. Place a walnut half (if using) on top of each muffin and bake for 30 minutes. Let them cool in the tin before popping them out.

Quinoa blueberry muffins

Ashley Madden, St John's, Canada

Gluten-free • Makes 6

extra virgin olive oil, for greasing

1 ripe banana

⅓ cup plant-based milk
  (I prefer almond)

3 tablespoons maple syrup

½ teaspoon vanilla extract

⅓ cup quinoa flour

½ cup quinoa flakes

½ cup rolled (porridge) oats

3 tablespoons hemp seeds

1 teaspoon ground cinnamon

½ teaspoon Himalayan salt or sea salt

2 teaspoons baking powder

1 teaspoon baking soda

1 cup fresh or frozen blueberries

Flax eggs

2 tablespoons flaxseed meal

75 ml (2¼ fl oz) warm water

Preheat the oven to 180°C (350°F/gas 4). Grease a muffin tin with a little extra virgin olive oil, or use muffin liners.

To make the flax eggs, place the flaxseed meal in a bowl and mix in the water. Let it sit for at least 5 minutes.

Combine the banana, milk, maple syrup, flax eggs and vanilla extract in a blender and blend until smooth. (You can also use a hand-held blender or go old-school and mix by hand yourself.)

In a large bowl, combine the quinoa flour and flakes, oats, hemp seeds, cinnamon, salt, baking powder and baking soda. Mix in the blueberries (if using frozen, don't wait too long to get them into the muffin tin or the batter will turn blue; but there's nothing wrong with blue muffins).

Slowly add the wet ingredients to the dry ingredients, mixing until just combined. Pour the batter into the greased muffin tin and bake for 25–28 minutes until golden brown on top and firm to touch. Let the muffins cool in the tin for 20–30 minutes. I use a narrow spatula to help pop them out. These muffins are moist and dense; be careful removing them.

NOTE: Buckwheat flour also works well or, if gluten isn't an issue, use wholemeal (whole-wheat) flour. You can buy quinoa flakes and flour in the organic/health food section of most grocery stores and at health food or bulk food stores.

Naan

Hester Dekker, Vught, The Netherlands
Makes 4

1⅔ cups plain (all-purpose) flour
¾ cup soy yoghurt
2 teaspoons dried yeast
½ teaspoon sea salt
2 garlic cloves, peeled and minced
2 tablespoons chopped coriander (cilantro)
1–2 teaspoons nigella seeds, plus extra to sprinkle on top

Preheat the oven to 220°C (425°F/gas 7).

Place all the ingredients in a bowl and knead very well for 10 minutes. Leave to rise in a warm place for 1 hour. Divide the dough into four pieces; roll out into thin triangles, brush with a little water, then sprinkle some extra nigella seeds on top. Bake in the middle of the oven for 5–8 minutes until golden and slightly risen. Enjoy warm.

 TIP: The dough and the baked naan can both be kept in the freezer.

 If you have the space, buy a bread-making machine and make your own bread, pizza dough, etc. That way, you will always know that no dairy product has been part of its preparation.
Jill Pack, London, United Kingdom

Avocado cornbread

Jack McNulty, Zurich, Switzerland

Makes 12–16 squares

75 ml (2¼ fl oz) extra virgin olive oil, plus extra for greasing

1 cup polenta bramata (coarse cornmeal)

175 g (6 oz) plain (all-purpose) flour

¼ cup masa flour (masa harina)

4 teaspoons baking powder

2 teaspoons sea salt

½ avocado, mashed

1 tablespoon flaxseed meal

2 teaspoons white wine or apple vinegar

425 ml (15 fl oz) rice milk

1½ tablespoons honey

Preheat your oven to 180°C (350°F/gas 4). Generously coat a baking tin (I use a 20 × 30 cm [8 × 12 inch] stainless steel tin) with extra virgin olive oil.

In a large bowl, mix together the polenta, flours, baking powder and salt. In a separate bowl, combine the mashed avocado, flaxseed meal and vinegar. Mix in the olive oil.

Combine the rice milk and honey in a jug, then add to the avocado mixture.

Add the wet ingredients to the dry ingredients and stir until just mixed together. Pour the batter into the prepared baking tin and bake until golden on top and a toothpick inserted in the centre comes out clean, 35–40 minutes. Cool slightly, then slice into squares.

TIPS: I like to store any leftover cornbread on a plate with a paper towel draped over the top (storing it in an airtight container makes it go mushy).

Masa flour is available from Mexican and good grocery stores.

Vegan biscuits

Jack McNulty, Zurich, Switzerland

Makes about 12 little biscuits

250 g (9 oz) plain (all-purpose) flour, plus extra for dusting

4 teaspoons rice starch or cornflour (cornstarch)

3 teaspoons baking powder

3 tablespoons sugar

1 teaspoon salt

3½ tablespoons extra virgin olive oil

150 ml (5 fl oz) plant-based milk (I prefer rice)

1 teaspoon white wine or apple cider vinegar

Vegan egg wash

4 tablespoons soy milk mixed with

2 tablespoons extra virgin olive oil

Preheat your oven to 220°C (425°F/gas 7). Line a baking tray with baking paper.

To make the vegan egg wash, combine the soy milk, oil and enough water to make a fluid mixture—it should be the same consistency as beaten egg. Set aside.

Combine the dry ingredients in a bowl, then sift twice to make sure everything is evenly distributed. Add the oil and mix well to combine, then work slightly with your fingers to create a polenta-like texture.

Combine the milk and vinegar and allow to stand for 5 minutes.

Mix the soured milk into the flour and oil mixture (you may need to add just a bit more flour if the mixture is too wet to handle—it should be moist but not overly sticky).

Place the dough on a well-floured surface and knead slightly, then flatten and roll out until the dough is roughly 1 cm (½ inch) thick. Cut out 5 cm (2 inch) rounds and place on the prepared tray. Brush the tops with the vegan egg wash and bake the biscuits for 13–16 minutes until lightly golden on top. Cool completely and enjoy right away.

NOTE: The biscuits are very similar to scones and are normally savoury. They are usually served with some sort of gravy, similar to how a dumpling might be served.

Baguette

Jack McNulty, Zurich, Switzerland

Makes 2 × 350 g (12 oz) baguettes

500 g (1 lb 2 oz) plain (all-purpose) flour, plus extra for dusting

2 teaspoons dried yeast

2 teaspoons sugar

285 ml (10 fl oz) warm water

2 teaspoons sea salt

extra virgin olive oil, for greasing

Sift the flour into the bowl of an electric mixer and form a deep well. Add the yeast, sugar and most of the water and mix with a dough hook attachment on speed number 2 until the dough comes together. Add the salt and continue to mix for 8–10 minutes.

Coat a large bowl very lightly with olive oil, add the dough and cover with a clean tea towel (dish towel). Set aside to prove in a warm spot—about 27°C (80°F)—for 1–1½ hours. The dough should leave an impression when pressed and it should come slowly back to form. Place the dough on a floured surface and fold in all sides to deflate the dough and force out the gas.

Divide the dough into two equal portions, then form each into a ball. Cover with a tea towel and rest for 10 minutes. Shape the baguettes by flattening each ball and rolling smoothly with the palms of your hands. Make sure to roll so the ends are slightly tapered. Place on a baking tray lined with baking paper, cover with a tea towel and set aside to prove for about 30 minutes.

Preheat the oven to 220°C (425°F/gas 7).

Use a bottle to spray the bread lightly with water, then make three diagonal slices in each baguette. Lightly dust with flour and bake for 30 minutes until a very deep golden colour, making sure you spray water into the oven three times during the first 3–5 minutes. Rest the bread on a wire rack for at least 1 hour, before slicing into it—just resist the temptation!

NOTE: This is an excellent recipe for beginners who want to explore the world of bread making, as it uses minimal ingredients and is a very basic straight dough method.

Chickpea piecrust

Claes Nermark, Helsingborg, Sweden

Gluten-free • Serves 4–6

250 g (9 oz) canned chickpeas (garbanzo beans), rinsed and drained
2 tablespoons extra virgin olive oil
3 tablespoons buckwheat flour
1 tablespoon water, if needed

Preheat the oven to 170°C (325°F/gas 3).

Combine the chickpeas, olive oil and buckwheat flour in a food processor and pulse until they come together to form a ball. (If this doesn't happen, add the tablespoon of water.)

Push the dough into a 20–23 cm (8–9 inch) pie dish with your fingers, pressing into the bottom and working your way up the side. Try to even out the dough so it isn't thick in some places. Prick the crust with a fork and bake for 15–20 minutes until a light golden colour. The crust is ready for the filling of your choice.

SWEETS

Strawberry mousse

Sandra Perry, Auckland, New Zealand

Serves 2

225 g (8 oz) silken tofu, drained
450 g (1 lb) strawberries, hulled and roughly chopped
finely grated zest of 1 orange
1 teaspoon honey

Place the tofu and strawberries in a blender. Reserve some of the orange zest strips for decoration and put the remaining zest in the blender with the honey. Process until smooth. Spoon the mousse into dessert dishes and chill. Decorate with the reserved orange zest.

 After experimenting a lot, I found silken tofu to be the best substitute for baking. Once mixed with a beater, it creates a nice, creamy mixture and gives a perfect consistency to all my cakes. (Silken tofu varies considerably in texture, so you may have to try some different brands until you find the one that works best.)

Annelise Friend, Mosman Park, Australia

Chocolate mousse

Wendy Wood, Murchison, New Zealand

Serves 6

8 dates, pitted and roughly chopped (if dried, soak in warm water for 20 minutes, then drain)

3 tablespoons orange juice

2 large, just ripe avocados

½ cup plant-based milk

3 tablespoons honey

½ teaspoon vanilla extract

3 tablespoons cacao powder

3 tablespoons chopped toasted almonds or hazelnuts, to decorate

Whiz the dates and orange juice in a food processor until smooth. Add the avocado, plant-based milk, honey, vanilla and cacao and process until very smooth. Divide between six serving cups or bowls and chill. When you're ready to serve dessert, top with the chopped nuts to serve.

 Stuff some fresh medjool dates with almond butter to have as a treat instead of cake. They're very rich and delicious, so you only need one or two.

Molly Greenwood, London, United Kingdom

Banana soft serve

Various versions submitted by multiple OMSers: Jane-Marie Harrison, Jenny Nicholson, Gili Ginossar, Alexandra

Serves 2

Base

2 ripe bananas, frozen for at least 6 hours or overnight

Berry soft serve

1 cup frozen berries

5 drops of vanilla extract

3 tablespoons plant-based milk

10 mint leaves

Chocolate soft serve

1 teaspoon cacao powder

1 handful of nuts (almonds, cashews or hazelnuts)

3 tablespoons plant-based milk

pinch of ground cinnamon

Almond soft serve

1 tablespoon almond butter

pinch of ground cinnamon

dash of almond extract (optional)

The frozen banana forms the base of your soft serve. Choose a flavour—berry, chocolate or almond—then put the frozen banana and the ingredients for that flavour into a food processor and process. When fully blended, serve immediately.

TIP: If you like this recipe, make sure you always have ripe bananas in the freezer.

Rhubarb sorbet

Wendy Wood, Murchison, New Zealand

Serves 8–10

500 g (1 lb 2 oz) rhubarb, trimmed, cut into 2 cm (¾ inch) pieces
200 g (7 oz) sugar
200 ml (7 fl oz) sugar syrup (½ cup hot water added to 125 g (4½ oz) sugar and
   stirred until dissolved)

Mix the rhubarb with the sugar and place in a saucepan over low heat. Cover and bring to a simmer, stirring often, until the rhubarb is soft and tender. Cool, then purée.

Add enough of the sugar syrup to the rhubarb to balance the acidity of the fruit so you get a nice sweet and sour flavour. Churn in an ice-cream machine; or freeze overnight then, using a fork, scrape up the frozen purée and process in a food processor until it resembles creamy, slushy snow. Pour into a suitable container, cover with baking paper and a lid and place in the freezer for at least 3 hours before serving with an ice-cream scoop or a tablespoon.

TIP: If the rhubarb is not very pink, replace some of the rhubarb with raspberries or freeze-dried raspberry powder.

Tiramisu

Hester Dekker, Vught, The Netherlands

Serves 6–8

200 ml (7 fl oz) cold espresso coffee

100 ml (3½ fl oz) amaretto

cacao powder, sifted, for dusting

Sponge fingers

4 egg whites

pinch of sea salt

100 g (3½ oz) sugar

1 heaped teaspoon vanilla sugar
  (see the tip on page 247)

3 tablespoons cornflour (cornstarch)

½ cup plain (all-purpose) or
  wholemeal (whole-wheat) flour

½ teaspoon baking powder

Cream

400 g (14 oz) silken tofu, drained

90 g (3¼ oz) sugar

1½ teaspoons vanilla sugar (see the
  tip on page 247)

Preheat the oven to 180°C (350°F/gas 4). Line a baking tray with baking paper.

To make the sponge fingers, whisk the egg whites, salt, sugar and vanilla sugar in a large bowl until the sugar dissolves and stiff peaks form. Sift in the cornflour, flour and baking powder and stir gently. Spoon the batter into a piping (icing) bag with a plain nozzle, or use a snap-lock bag and cut a 1–1.5 cm (½–⅝ inch) diameter hole in one corner. Squeeze 2 × 8 cm (¾ × 3¼ inch) strips of batter onto the prepared tray and bake for 10–15 minutes until the sponge fingers start to brown.

To make the cream, combine the silken tofu, sugar and vanilla sugar in a blender or food processor and process until really smooth.

In a shallow bowl, mix the espresso and amaretto. Add the sponge fingers and soak for a few minutes. They should not fall apart, but should be well soaked.

Take a large shallow dish and put down a layer of soaked sponge fingers, then add half the cream, a second layer of sponge fingers and the rest of the cream. Put the dish in the refrigerator for at least several hours to set. Dust the tiramisu with the cacao just before serving.

TIP: To make vanilla sugar, cut a vanilla bean in half and place it in a jar with 100 g (3½ oz) caster (superfine) sugar. Leave it for 1 week before using; the longer you keep it, the stronger the flavour will be.

Poppy seed strudel

Stephanie Pielot, Southampton, United Kingdom

Serves 6–8

Dough

200 g (7 oz) wholemeal (whole-wheat)
   plain (all-purpose) flour (or any other
   flour)

⅓ cup wholemeal (whole-wheat) spelt
   flour

3 tablespoons sugar

pinch of sea salt

2 teaspoons dried yeast

135 ml (4½ fl oz) plant-based milk

pinch of vanilla powder or a dash of
   vanilla extract

2 tablespoons extra virgin olive oil

juice of ½ lemon

Filling

1 cup plant-based milk

3 tablespoons agave nectar

1½ tablespoons maple syrup

150 g (5½ oz) poppy seeds, ground in
   a food processor

pinch of vanilla powder or a dash of
   vanilla extract

1–2 tablespoons cornflour (cornstarch)

To make the dough, mix the dry ingredients in a bowl and combine the milk, vanilla and olive oil in a separate bowl. Slowly stir the wet ingredients into the dry ingredients, then add the lemon juice (if you mix the lemon with the wet ingredients the milk will curdle). Knead the dough thoroughly—the longer you knead the better. Leave the dough to rise in a warm place until doubled in size, 1–2 hours.

Preheat the oven to 160°C (315°C/gas 2–3).

Prepare the filling. In a saucepan, bring the milk, agave nectar, maple syrup, poppy seeds and vanilla to the boil, turn down the heat and simmer for a few minutes. Mix the cornflour with a little cold water to make a runny paste, then pour into the poppy seed milk. Boil once again to thicken. Take off the heat and cool a little. The filling should have a spreadable consistency similar to apple sauce or jam.

Roll out the dough to 1–2 cm (½–¾ inch) thick. Spread on the poppy seed filling and roll up. Bake for about 30 minutes until golden.

Strawberry mousse cake

Lucie Williams, Paraparaumu, New Zealand

Serves 8

raspberries, to decorate (optional)

Base
1½ cups almond meal
2 tablespoons extra virgin olive oil
1 tablespoon honey
2 tablespoons water

Filling
2 egg whites, at room temperature
¾ cup sugar
250 g (9 oz) strawberries, hulled and
  sliced
1 tablespoon lemon juice
1 teaspoon vanilla extract

Preheat the oven to 180°C (350°F/gas 4). Line the base of a 20 cm (8 inch) springform cake tin with baking paper.

Combine all the base ingredients in a food processor and pulse until the mixture resembles coarse crumbs. Tip into the prepared tin and press evenly onto the base. Bake for 10 minutes, or until golden brown. Remove from the oven and leave to cool completely.

Place the filling ingredients in the bowl of an electric mixer and beat on low speed and then on high speed for 6–8 minutes until the mixture is very thick and the sugar has dissolved.

Spread the filling over the cooled base, cover with a sheet of baking paper and freeze for at least 6 hours. Remove the cake from the freezer about 5–10 minutes before serving, to make lifting out of the tin easier. Cut with a warm knife. Serve with the raspberries on top, if desired.

TIP: You can use frozen strawberries for this recipe but, after you've thawed them, make sure to drain and pat them dry.

Pineapple cake

Josephine van der Wel, Frenchville, Australia

Serves 8–10

2 cups plain (all-purpose) flour
2 teaspoons baking powder
½ cup sugar
450 g (1 lb) canned crushed pineapple with juice

Preheat the oven to 180°C (350°F/gas 4). Line a 23 × 13 cm (9 × 5 inch) cake tin with baking paper.

Sift the flour and baking powder into a bowl, then add the sugar and stir to combine. Add the pineapple (the entire contents of the can with juice) and mix well. Pour into the cake tin and bake for 40–50 minutes. It will be ready when a skewer inserted in the centre comes out clean. Let the cake cool in the tin before turning it out.

Bitter orange cacao cake

Jane-Marie Harrison, Beech Cottage, United Kingdom

Gluten-free • Serves 12

375 g (13 oz) clementines or oranges
175 g (6 oz) soft dark brown sugar
3 dessertspoons cacao powder
2½ cups almond meal
8 egg whites
1 heaped tablespoon baking powder

Boil the whole clementines or oranges with the skin on for 2 hours. Drain and allow to cool. Cut in half and remove any pips.

Preheat the oven to 190°C (375°C/gas 5). Grease a 20 cm (8 inch) springform cake tin and line the base and side with baking paper.

Pulp the fruit in its entirety (with skins on) in a food processor. Add the sugar and cacao and whiz until smooth. Add the almond meal and pulse to combine.

Beat the egg whites to stiff peaks in a large bowl, then fold into the orange mixture together with the baking powder. Pour into the prepared tin, heaping slightly in the centre as the cake tends to sink a little after baking. Bake the cake for 40 minutes, cover with foil to prevent the top from burning and bake for a further 20 minutes. I find the cake sometimes needs a bit longer to cook, an extra 10 minutes or so. I think it depends on the juice content of the fruit. A skewer comes out clean when the cake is cooked.

TIPS: Some people say the cake is best eaten the day after baking. I'm happy to eat it as soon as it is cool!

I sometimes serve this cake as a dessert, hot with custard or cold with cream (soy, of course!).

Apple cinnamon upside-down cake

Ingrid Adelsberger, Los Angeles, United States

Serves 8–10

2 gala apples, cored and thinly sliced

2 teaspoons soft brown sugar, to sprinkle (optional)

1¾ cups plain (all-purpose) flour or pastry flour

2 teaspoons baking powder

1½ teaspoons ground cinnamon

½ teaspoon sea salt

2 tablespoons extra virgin olive oil

½ cup sugar

⅔ cup soy milk

2 tablespoons vanilla extract

1 tablespoon apple cider vinegar

Preheat the oven to 180°C (350°F/gas 4). Line a 20 cm (8 inch) round cake tin with baking paper.

Arrange the apple slices in a single layer on the base of the prepared tin and sprinkle with the brown sugar (if using).

In a bowl, sift together the flour, baking powder and cinnamon.

In a separate smaller bowl, whisk the salt, olive oil, sugar, soy milk, vanilla and vinegar until blended.

Pour the wet mixture into the dry mixture, whisking until smooth. Pour the batter into the tin and bake for 30–40 minutes, or until a toothpick inserted in the centre comes out clean. Cool the cake in the tin for 5–10 minutes. Invert the cake onto a plate and cool.

Coffee cacao banana bread

Gili Ginossar, Jerusalem, Israel

Serves 8–10

2 teaspoons instant coffee
3 tablespoons boiling water
⅓ cup extra virgin olive oil
110 g (3¾ oz) apple sauce
2 tablespoons tahini
4 large ripe bananas, mashed
210 g (7½ oz) spelt flour
½ cup lightly packed soft brown sugar
1 teaspoon baking soda
3 tablespoons cacao powder
pinch of sea salt

Preheat the oven to 180°C (350°F/gas 4).

Combine the coffee and water in a bowl. Add the oil, apple sauce, tahini and mashed banana and mix well.

In a separate bowl, mix together the flour, sugar, baking soda, cacao and salt.

Now mix the wet and the dry ingredients together, but not too much. Pour into a greased 20 × 10 cm (8 × 4 inch) loaf (bar) tin and bake for 50 minutes. It will be ready when a skewer inserted in the centre comes out clean. Let the cake cool in the tin before turning it out.

Lemon meringue pie

Keryn Taylor, Carlton, Australia

Serves 12

Crust

1 cup rolled (porridge) oats

½ cup soft brown sugar

3 tablespoons extra virgin olive oil

Meringue

4 egg whites

½ cup caster (superfine) sugar

Lemon curd

1 cup sugar

⅔ cup soy milk

100 ml (3½ fl oz) orange juice (with pulp
  if you like)

¼ teaspoon sea salt

½ cup cornflour (cornstarch)

½ cup lemon juice

2 tablespoons finely grated lemon zest

Preheat the oven to 180°C (350°F/gas 4).

Process all the crust ingredients in a food processor and press into a 20 cm (8 inch) pie dish. Bake for 10 minutes and remove from the oven.

To make the lemon curd, combine the sugar, soy milk, orange juice and salt in a saucepan over medium heat and bring it to the boil, stirring, until the sugar dissolves. Whisk in the cornflour and continue to whisk until the mixture is thick. Remove from the heat and mix in the lemon juice and zest. Pour the curd over the crust.

Beat the egg whites in a large bowl until soft peaks form, then slowly add the sugar, whisking to form a thick meringue.

Spoon the meringue over the curd, making peaks. Bake for 10–15 minutes until the meringue is lightly browned. Set aside to cool, then refrigerate.

TIP: If you want to reduce the amount of sugar in this pie, you can halve the sugar in the crust and curd but not in the meringue, as you need the sugar for consistency and stability.

Christmas cake

Abba Renshaw, Auckland, New Zealand

Serves 12

2 cups strong black coffee
1 kg (2 lb 4 oz) mixed dried fruit
2 cups self-raising flour

Pour the coffee on the fruit, cover and leave overnight.

Preheat the oven to 160°C (315°F/gas 2–3).

Mix the flour into the coffee and fruit. Spoon into a 20 cm (8 inch) round cake tin and bake for 1¾–2 hours until a skewer inserted in the centre comes out clean. Leave it in the tin to cool before turning it out onto a plate.

 To make aquafaba ('water-bean'), an egg white substitute, save the liquid from chickpea (garbanzo bean) cans or from homemade chickpeas. It whips up into a meringue-like consistency and can replace eggs in most baked goods (use 3 tablespoons aquafaba per egg). For future baking, freeze it in ice-cube trays, 1 tablespoon per cube.

Sherida Deeprose, Adliswil, Switzerland

Irish whiskey cake

Jessica van Esch, County Kerry, Ireland

Serves 8–10

300 g (10½ oz) sultanas (golden raisins) or a mix of glacé cherries, sultanas, raisins and currants

175 g (6 oz) sugar (can be a mix of white and brown if desired)

1 tablespoon whiskey

300 ml (10½ fl oz) cold tea

2 egg whites

300 g (10½ oz) self-raising flour

3 tablespoons honey (or more) or 3–4 tablespoons whiskey (optional)

Glaze

½ cup icing (confectioners') sugar

1 tablespoon orange juice

Mix the sultanas or glacé and dried fruit, sugar, whiskey and tea in a large bowl and set aside to soak for at least 24 hours, up to 48 hours, until all the tea has been absorbed into the fruit.

Preheat the oven to 180°C (350°F/gas 4). Grease a 20 cm (8 inch) cake tin, or line a muffin tin with paper cases.

Stir the egg whites, then the flour, into the fruit mixture and beat thoroughly with a wooden spoon until well mixed. Pour into the prepared tin and bake the cake for 1½ hours or the cupcakes for 40 minutes. The cake/s are ready when a skewer inserted in the centre comes out clean. If you want, prick the top of the cake/s and drizzle the honey or whiskey over the top while still hot. Allow to stand for 5 minutes, then remove from the tin and place on a wire rack.

To make the glaze, whisk the sugar and orange juice in a small bowl until smooth, then brush on top of the cake/s while still warm.

Cacao bean brownies

Jenny Nicholson, Oxford, United Kingdom

Makes 16 squares

½ cup cacao powder, plus extra for dusting

1–2 cups pitted dates (depending on desired sweetness)

1 teaspoon vanilla extract

2 tablespoons almond butter

3 cups cooked black beans (or 2 × 400 g [14 oz] cans black beans, drained and rinsed)

½ teaspoon sea salt

1 cup chopped walnuts (optional)

1 teaspoon almond extract (optional)

raspberries or other berries, to decorate

1 teaspoon agave nectar mixed with 1 teaspoon cacao powder, to drizzle (optional)

Preheat the oven to 100°C (200°F/gas ½). Line a 20 cm (8 inch) square baking tin with baking paper and dust with the extra cacao powder.

Process the dates, vanilla and almond butter in a food processor until you have a creamy paste. Add the black beans and process to combine. Scoop the mixture into a bowl and add the cacao powder and salt. Knead with your hands to mix. Now is the time to add the walnuts and almond extract (if using).

Spread the batter in the prepared tin, pressing down firmly, and bake for 1½ hours, or until the brownie has a nicely baked surface. Cool completely before slicing into small squares.

Decorate with the berries and drizzle with the agave nectar mixed with cacao, if you like.

Baked apples

Jane-Marie Harrison, Beech Cottage, United Kingdom

Serves 6

6 medium bramley apples (or another tart apple, such as granny smith)
2 tablespoons almond meal
plump raisins (quantity depends on the size of your apples)
2 teaspoons ground allspice
2 tablespoons chopped pitted dates
2 tablespoons brandy, apple juice or orange juice, to bind

Preheat the oven to 160°C (315°F/gas 2–3).

Core the apples but keep the bottom 1 cm (½ inch) or so of the core to use as a plug. Fix this back into the bottom of the apple to stop the filling from escaping. Score round the middle of the apple to allow for expansion as the apples bake.

Mix together the almond meal, raisins, allspice and dates and bind with the chosen liquid. Spoon the filling into the centre of the apples. Put on a baking tray and bake for around 30 minutes until the apples are tender.

TIPS: These look and smell just like little Christmas puddings! If served at Christmas, decorate with small sprigs of holly.

You may need to adjust the cooking time if the apples are small or large.

Chestnut cacao fondant

Gaspar Hoyos, Nancy, France
Serves 4; makes 350 g (12 oz) chestnut cream

1 tablespoon cacao powder
40 g (1½ oz) almond butter
plant-based milk, if needed
3 egg whites
50 g (1¾ oz) sugar

Chestnut cream
200 g (7 oz) precooked chestnuts
½ cup plant-based milk
2½ tablespoons icing (confectioners') sugar
1 teaspoon vanilla extract
1 teaspoon kirsch (or vodka or schnapps)

Preheat the oven to 180°C (350°F/gas 4). Line a 20 cm (8 inch) square baking tin with baking paper.

To make the chestnut cream, cook the chestnuts in your favourite plant-based milk until soft. (The cooking time will depend on whether you're using fresh or canned chestnuts.) Add the sugar, vanilla and kirsch and stir well. Continue to cook for about 5 minutes. Remove from the heat and purée in a high-speed blender. Adjust with water if it is too thick. It should fall off your spoon in clumps like creamy potato mash.

Mix together the cacao, almond butter and chestnut cream. If the mixture is too solid (it depends on the almond butter texture), add some plant-based milk of your preference. It should be a creamy consistency.

Whisk the egg whites and sugar in a large bowl until thick and glossy. Fold the cacao, almond butter and chestnut cream mixture into the egg white, spoon into the prepared tin and bake for 20–25 minutes. Enjoy it warm from the oven, or cool before serving.

Blondie

Ingrid Adelsberger, Los Angeles, United States

Makes 12 squares

extra virgin olive oil

425 g (15 oz) can chickpeas (garbanzo beans), rinsed and drained

⅓ cup almond butter

3 tablespoons maple syrup or agave nectar

2 tablespoons plant-based milk

2 teaspoons vanilla extract

½ teaspoon sea salt

½ teaspoon baking powder

¼ cup coarsely chopped cashews or nuts of your choice
  (for some texture)

Preheat the oven to 180°C (350°F/gas 4) and spray a 20 cm (8 inch) square baking tin with a little extra virgin olive oil.

Put all the ingredients except the nuts into a food processor and blend to a smooth batter. Spread the batter evenly in the prepared tin and sprinkle the ground nuts on top. Bake for 20–25 minutes until the edges are a tiny bit brown and a toothpick inserted in the centre comes out clean. The batter may not look cooked, but it will be fine!

Cool in the tin before cutting into squares.

Fruit crumble

Patrick Manning, Bolton, United Kingdom

Serves 8

680 g (1 lb 8 oz) fruit (such as plums, gooseberries, rhubarb, apple and
  blackberries), peeled, cored and chopped
sweetener of choice

Topping
115 g (4 oz) rolled (porridge) oats
¾ cup spelt flour
¼ cup almond meal
1½ teaspoons baking powder
⅓ cup soft brown sugar
2 tablespoons extra virgin olive oil

Place the fruit in a saucepan, add a little water and bring to the boil. Sweeten to taste; I use maple syrup or agave nectar. Turn off the heat before the fruit turns to mush.

Preheat the oven to 170°C (325°F/gas 3) fan-forced.

To make the topping, put the oats, spelt flour, almond meal, baking powder and sugar in a food processor and blitz. I use the plastic blade to try and keep the oats as big as possible. Drizzle in the olive oil while processing. How much to use? You'll need to be able to tip it out of the processor and shake it over the fruit.

Put the hot fruit and liquid into your favourite ovenproof crumble dish. Tip out the topping as evenly as possible over the fruit and press down. Bake on the top shelf in the oven for 25–30 minutes.

Orange cake

Ingrid Adelsberger, Los Angeles, United States

Serves 6–8

1 cup wholemeal (whole-wheat) plain (all-purpose) flour

pinch of sea salt

½ teaspoon baking powder

½ teaspoon baking soda

½ cup icing (confectioners') sugar, plus more if required

3 tablespoons extra virgin olive oil

1 cup orange juice (or use 3–4 peeled oranges, processed in a food processor
   and strained)

½ teaspoon finely grated orange zest

Preheat your oven to 180°C (350°F/gas 4). Line an 18 × 10 cm (7 × 4 inch) baking tin with baking paper.

Sift the flour, salt, baking powder and baking soda into a bowl.

In another bowl, combine the sugar and olive oil and, using an electric mixer, hand beater or wooden spoon, beat until creamy. Add the orange juice and stir very well, then stir in the orange zest. Add the dry ingredients. There should be no lumps in the batter.

Pour the batter into the prepared tin and use a spatula to scrape any batter from the side of the bowl. Tap the sides of the tin to release the air bubbles and even out the batter. Bake for 30–35 minutes. This cake keeps well in the fridge for 3–4 days.

Butternut pumpkin cake

Gaspar Hoyos, Nancy, France

Serves 8

500 g (1 lb 2 oz) butternut pumpkin (squash), grated
150 g (5½ oz) sugar
280 g (10 oz) plain (all-purpose) flour
2 teaspoons baking powder
⅔ cup extra virgin olive oil
4 egg whites
lemon zest
1 handful of raisins (optional)
1 handful of chopped almonds

Mix the pumpkin with the sugar in a bowl. Mix in the flour and baking powder. While still mixing, add the oil and egg whites and finally fold in the lemon zest, raisins (if using) and almonds.

Pour the batter into a greased 23 cm (9 inch) round cake tin. Bake at 200°C (400°F/gas 6), without preheating the oven, for 20–25 minutes.

 VARIATIONS: Use carrots instead of butternut pumpkin.
You can also make muffins using a muffin tin. Bake for 15–20 minutes.

Sweet hazelnut and apple snails

Silvia Gautschi McNulty, Zurich, Switzerland

Makes 26

apricot jam (enough to coat the dough before adding the hazelnut filling, so best to have a jar on hand)

Dough

500 g (1 lb 2 oz) plain (all-purpose) flour

15 g (½ oz) fresh yeast or 2 teaspoons dried yeast

90 g (3¼ oz) sugar

3 tablespoons extra virgin olive oil

300 ml (10½ fl oz) plant-based milk (rice or oat work best)

½ tablespoon sea salt

Filling

150 g (5½ oz) ground hazelnuts

heaped ¼ cup raisins

⅓ cup sugar

4 tablespoons lemon juice

4 tablespoons plant-based milk

140 g (5 oz) grated apple

zest of ½ lemon

pinch of ground cinnamon

Icing

½ cup icing (confectioners') sugar

1 tablespoon lemon juice

2 tablespoons water

Make the dough first by combining the flour, yeast, sugar, olive oil and plant-based milk in a bowl. Mix and knead the dough for 2 minutes. Add the salt and continue to knead for 7 minutes. The dough will be a bit wet, so resist adding too much flour . . . just add enough so the dough doesn't stick to the work surface. Place the dough in an oiled bowl, cover with plastic wrap and set aside in a warm spot to rise for 2 hours.

Meanwhile, mix all the filling ingredients together. Mix all the ingredients together for the icing.

Preheat the oven to 180°C (350°F/gas 4). Line a baking tray with baking paper.

When the dough is ready, divide into two even pieces. Roll each piece out into a rectangle, about ½ cm (¼ inch) thick. Coat each with a thin layer of apricot jam and half the filling, leaving a gap on the end furthest from you. Roll the dough up like a Swiss roll and cut into 4 cm (1½ inch) pieces. Put the slices on their sides and flatten a little bit. Place on the prepared tray and bake for 30 minutes. Remove from the oven, brush the icing on the snails while still hot and allow them to cool before eating.

Fig and pecan biscotti

Jo McCulloch, Blenheim, New Zealand

Makes about 30

4 egg whites

⅓ cup caster (superfine) sugar

1¼ cups sifted plain (all-purpose) flour

½ teaspoon baking powder

½ cup pecans

½ cup chopped dried figs

Preheat the oven to 180°C (350°F/gas 4). Line a baking tray with baking paper.

In a large bowl, whisk the egg whites and sugar for 5 minutes until thick and glossy. Fold in the flour, baking powder, pecans and figs. Do not overmix.

Shape the dough into a log about 1 cm (½ inch) thick and flatten it slightly. Bake for 18 minutes. Cool on a wire rack for 20 minutes, then slice it diagonally into ½ cm (¼ inch) slices.

Lay the slices on the lined baking tray, then put the tray back in the oven for 15–20 minutes until both sides of the biscotti are completely dry. Cool on a wire rack and store in an airtight container.

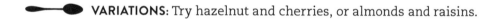

VARIATIONS: Try hazelnut and cherries, or almonds and raisins.

Chickpea shortbread

Jack McNulty, Zurich, Switzerland

Gluten-free • Makes 20 cookies

120 g (4¼ oz) caster (superfine) sugar

75 ml (2¼ fl oz) extra virgin olive oil

100 g (3½ oz) chickpea flour (besan)

100 g (3½ oz) gluten-free plain (all-purpose) flour

25 g (1 oz) rice flour or cornflour (cornstarch)

½ teaspoon baking powder

1½ teaspoons sea salt

3 teaspoons orange blossom water

finely grated zest of 1 lemon

4 tablespoons plant-based milk, plus extra if needed

Preheat the oven to 180°C (350°F/gas 4). Line a baking tray with baking paper.

Combine the sugar and oil in a bowl and mix with an electric mixer for about 2 minutes.

In a separate bowl, sift together the flours, baking powder and salt.

Add the flour mixture to the sugar and oil mixture. Mix in the orange blossom water, lemon zest and enough milk to get the dough to just hold together.

Roll out the dough on a work surface until 1 cm (½ inch) thick. Cut out circles or rectangles (you can re-roll the leftover dough) and poke some holes in the top with a fork. Place on the prepared tray and bake for 15 minutes.

Reduce the oven temperature to 160°C (315°F/gas 2–3) and continue to bake for 7–10 minutes. Cool the shortbread for a few minutes on the baking tray before transferring to a wire rack to cool completely.

Cavallucci di siena

Jack McNulty, Zurich, Switzerland

Makes 20 cookies

200 g (7 oz) caster (superfine) sugar
100 g (3½ oz) honey
500 g (1 lb 2 oz) plain (all-purpose) flour
1½ teaspoons baking soda
2 teaspoons anise seeds, crushed
100 g (3½ oz) candied orange, diced
8–10 walnuts, lightly toasted and chopped
pinch of sea salt
sifted icing (confectioners') sugar, to serve

Preheat the oven to 180°C (350°F/gas 4). Line a baking tray with baking paper.

Mix together the sugar and honey in a heavy-based saucepan and cook over low heat, stirring until the sugar is dissolved and a thick syrup is created.

Meanwhile, mix together the flour and baking soda and sift into a large bowl. Add the anise seeds, candied orange, nuts and salt and mix well to combine. Pour in the hot syrup and mix with a spoon. The dough should be a bit on the dry side. Go ahead and add a bit of water if you think it is too dry to work with (I sometimes add a plant-based milk to loosen up the dough).

Let the dough sit for about 5 minutes, then lightly roll it out into a log shape on a lightly floured or oiled surface. Slice into 2 cm (¾ inch) pieces and place on the prepared tray. Bake for about 20 minutes. Don't allow the cookies to brown too much . . . just check the bottom of one to see if it is hard and lightly golden. Immediately roll the cookies in the icing sugar and allow to cool. They will keep for about 1 week in an airtight container—but they rarely make it more than a day or two in our house.

Stem ginger macaroons

Jill Pack, London, United Kingdom

Makes about 25

2 cups almond meal
⅓ cup caster (superfine) sugar
2 egg whites
100 g (3½ oz) chopped stem ginger, minus the syrup
flaked almonds
icing (confectioners') sugar

Preheat the oven to 170°C (325°F/gas 3) or 150°C (300°F/gas 2) fan-forced. Line a baking tray with baking paper.

Mix the almond meal, sugar, egg whites and stem ginger until evenly combined. Roll into balls the size of a smallish walnut, then roll in a mound of flaked almonds, so a layer sticks to the outside. This is a bit messy, but doable.

Place the macaroons on the prepared tray, then bake for 25–30 minutes until golden brown. Sift the icing sugar over the top while they are hot and leave to cool.

Decadent cocoa cupcakes

Ingrid Adelsberger, Los Angeles, United States
Makes 12

Cupcakes
1 cup unsweetened almond milk
1 teaspoon apple cider vinegar
½ cup sugar (I use brown)
⅓ cup extra virgin olive oil
1½ teaspoons vanilla extract
1 cup wholemeal (whole-wheat) flour
⅓ cup unsweetened cocoa powder
¾ teaspoon baking soda
½ teaspoon baking powder
¼ teaspoon sea salt

Icing
2 ripe avocados, flesh scooped out
¼ cup unsweetened cocoa powder
3 tablespoons maple syrup
½ teaspoon vanilla extract

Preheat the oven to 180°C (350°F/gas 4). Grease a muffin tin or line it with 12 paper or silicone cups.

Whisk together the almond milk and apple cider vinegar and set aside for a few minutes while the milk curdles.

Beat in the sugar, oil and vanilla until foamy.

In a separate bowl, combine the flour, cocoa powder, baking soda, baking powder and salt, then slowly beat in the wet ingredients until smooth. Divide the batter evenly between the 12 cups.

Bake for 18–25 minutes, or until a toothpick inserted in the centre comes out clean. Remove the cupcakes from the oven, and after a few minutes, transfer them to a wire rack to cool.

While the cupcakes are baking, make the icing. Place the avocado flesh in a food processor. Add the cocoa powder, maple syrup and vanilla and purée until smooth.

Once the cupcakes have cooled, ice them. Even though they are OMS-friendly, these cupcakes are a bit high in saturated fat, so I bake them as a special treat for parties and birthdays. Everyone will love them.

AFTERWORD

I can honestly say that I learned a tremendous amount while working on this cookbook. There were many tricks I just didn't know, so my cooking skills have really improved over the past months. But, more importantly, on an emotional level, I feel very differently about my eating habits.

I've barely eaten out over the past months and I have to say I haven't missed it. I realised that the only times I drift from being 100 per cent OMS compliant are when I eat out. Eating at home means that I increase my chances of eating as well as I can.

I used to focus on 'what I could get away with'. These days when I socialise I meet friends for lunch, coffee or drinks, or invite them to my house so I provide the food. Where I live lunch seems a bit easier, as it is a smaller meal, so when eating out I just need to worry about finding a place that serves salads, a vegan soup, a smoked salmon sandwich, sushi or a grain/legume plate—all my go-to dishes.

Planning my life a bit differently has not been a huge compromise; in fact it has reduced or eliminated any failures to comply with the OMS diet. Also, having a cookbook like this that includes a range of recipes from various cuisines will help me not to miss dishes I could eat in the past.

When I started on the OMS diet I thought that 10 g (¼ oz) of saturated fat a day was very little. It seemed almost impossible to stay within that range. But that was because most things I was eating were processed and high in saturated fat. If I stick to the food groups that are recommended, 10 g (¼ oz) of saturated fat is actually quite a lot.

When I weighed serving sizes, many whole foods contained less fat than I thought. So, for instance, I'd been very careful with how much almond butter—and nuts in general—I consumed. In the US a 32 g (1 oz) serving size of almond butter—which is a lot!—has between 1–2 g (less than ¹⁄₁₆ oz) of saturated fat, depending on the brand. I had been using much less. Obviously, this will not make me change my eating habits but it helps to ease my worry that my diet is too high in saturated fat.

When looking at all the changes and improvements I made to my life and diet, I think not stressing about my saturated fat intake is probably the most important one. All I need to focus on is making choices from the healthy food groups.

It takes time for new behaviour to become habit, and this applies very much to OMS—the diet as well as the entire program. Be patient and give yourself the time you need to create these eating habits so they stick. Remember this is not a four-week program to lose weight; it's a permanent lifestyle choice to manage and improve your health and live a happy, healthy life.

ACKNOWLEDGEMENTS

Many people made this cookbook possible.

First and foremost, George Jelinek. George, without you there would be no Overcoming Multiple Sclerosis (OMS) program and therefore no OMS cookbook. I remember the first day of the OMS retreat in the UK—you were standing in the meeting room, chatting with others, and I thought, 'That's George, and his voice sounds exactly as it does on all the podcasts!' I often reflect on the fact that you have dedicated almost 20 years of your life to finding a way to empower people with MS so they can live a healthy, happy life. I am so grateful to you for sharing all your research online so people like me, all over the world, can access the information they need to improve their lives while potentially overcoming the disease.

Gary McMahon, Linda Bloom and everyone at OMS, thank you for listening to my idea and moving it forward so it landed with Allen & Unwin. Furthermore, thank you for your support with tapping into the OMS community and crowdsourcing recipes.

Jack McNulty, thank you for your advice and recipes. I've enjoyed every single discussion as well as many laughs during our Skype calls. Your expertise and knowledge has made this book much richer. You taught me many things, and so often when I cook these days I wonder, 'What would Jack suggest in this situation?'

Sandra Perry, thank you for contributing your expertise as a nutritionist, adding another layer of wisdom for our readers. It was wonderful to see the various recipes compiled together in your menu plan.

All our OMS contributors, thank you for submitting recipes. I couldn't have done it without all your wonderful dishes, based on cuisines from all over the world.

Elizabeth Weiss, Sarah Baker and everyone at Allen & Unwin who helped to publish the book. Elizabeth, thank you for your guidance and patience with my many questions as well as your precise and detailed work throughout the process. Sarah, thank you for all your work during the production of the book and also your warm, friendly emails and encouragement at every step.

My family—*Danke Mama, Vati und Gudrun für alles. Ich hab Euch sehr lieb!*

My friends, thank you for believing in me and this book. Your support and encouragement was so important through the difficult times that accompany such a big project. So many of you supported me with words, emails or messages from abroad as well as all sorts of ideas, not to mention your courage in taste-testing recipes during the selection process. You all know who you are!!!

Last, but certainly not least, my husband and best friend, Dat. You believed in this book from the zero hour, even before I did. Without your encouragement I may have never written to George about my cookbook idea. Thank you for your loving push every time I had doubts. You helped with grocery shopping so many times over the months, taste-tested almost every recipe with me and never complained when I put a meal in front of you. There are no words to describe how much I appreciated your loving support at every step along the path.

INDEX

A

abbreviations 31
Adelsberger, Ingrid ix–x, 2, 5–7, 270–1
African food 27
    Ghanaian fish stew 190
    Moroccan-style fish stew 191
    Moroccan-style vegetable stew 199
allergies 34
almonds *see also* nuts
    Almond butter and goji berry flapjacks 58
    Almond cream sauce 156
    Almond shaker 230
    Almond soft serve 244
    Pesto almonds 51
Angel's eggs 72
apple
    Apple cinnamon upside-down cake 252
    Apple quinoa breakfast 37
    Baked apples 258
    Sweet hazelnut and apple snails 264
aquafaba 255
Asian food 27–8
asparagus
    Lemon asparagus 210
aubergine *see* eggplant
Autumn glory 198
avocado
    Avocado cornbread 237
    Creamy avocado pasta with prawns 182
    Sweet potato and avocado soup 108
    Tuna with avocado salad 77

B

Baba ghanoush 64
Baguette 239
Baked apple 258
Baked crusted cod 139
Baked fruit and nut clusters 53
Baked salmon in maple mustard sauce 137
Baked tofu 115
Baked wasabi edamame 59

baking 24
Balkan rice 176
Balsamic dressing 228
Banana
    Banana ginger apple muffins 234
    Banana soft serve 244
Barbecue sauce 215
bars
    Breakfast bars 45
    Peppermint bars 52
Basic vegetable stock 110
beans/legumes 20
    Bean dip 66
    Black bean and beetroot burgers 169–70
    Blondie 260
    Broccoli and chickpea burgers 166
    Chickpea piecrust 240
    Chickpea salad with mint 82
    Chickpea shortbread 266
    Chickpea stew with silverbeet 197
    Haricot bean and watercress soup 103
    Honey-mustard glazed green beans 206
    Indian-spiced chickpeas 151
    Indian-style curried split pea soup 109
    Ingrid's favourite macro plate 177
    Lentil bolognese 178
    Lentil-mushroom burgers 168
    Mexican black bean salad 84
    Moroccan-style vegetable stew 199
    Potato quinoa patties with chickpea curry
        149–50
    Prawn and pea egg white frittata 144
    Sugar snap peas with mint 207
    Sweet and sour haricot beans 153
    Tarka dal 179
    Tuna and cannellini bean salad 80
    Vegan split pea and sweet potato soup 111
    Vegetable protein burgers 171
    Warm bok choy, prawn and lentil salad 194
beetroot
    Beetroot and walnut salad 79

Black bean and beetroot burgers 169–70
Berry soft serve 244
bhajis
    Onion bhajis 71
biscuits *see also* sweets
    Baked fruit and nut clusters 53
    Fig and pecan biscotti 265
    Olive oil crackers 54
    Salty sesame biscuits 50
    Vegan biscuits 238
Bitter orange cacao cake 251
Black bean and beetroot burgers 169
Blondie 260
Blueberry pancakes 39
boiling 24–5
bok choy
    Warm bok choy, prawn and lentil salad 194
bread
    Avocado cornbread 237
    Baguette 239
    bread-making machine 236
    Coffee cacao banana bread 253
    Naan 236
breakfast
    Apple quinoa breakfast 37
    Blueberry pancakes 39
    Breakfast bars 45
    Breakfast burrito 41
    Egg white omelette 46–7
    Granola 43
    Kousmine-Budwig breakfast 36
    Oat-flour crepes 38
    Overnight oatmeal 44
    Scrambled tofu 40
    Tropical chia breakfast bowl 42
broccoli
    Broccoli and chickpea burgers 166
    Broccoli and mushroom quiche with
        wholegrain garlic crust 158–9
    Cheesy-baked broccoli 208
    Cream of broccoli soup 100
    Noémie's pie 160
    Smoked salmon, broccoli and lemon
        pasta 186
brussels sprouts
    Steamed brussels sprouts and tahini dill
        sauce 202
    Sweet potato and brussels sprout gratin 156

burgers
    Black bean and beetroot 169–70
    Broccoli and chickpea 166
    Lentil-mushroom 168
    Salmon 167
    Vegetable protein 171
burghul
    Zucchini and burghul salad 90
burrito
    Breakfast burrito 41
butter substitutes 12
Butternut pumpkin and white fish
    curry 192
Butternut pumpkin cake 263

C
cacao
    Bitter orange cacao cake 251
    Cacao bean brownies 257
    Chestnut cacao fondant 259
    Coffee cacao banana bread 253
cakes *see* sweets
calamari *see also* fish and shellfish
Calamari with turmeric and garlic 140
capsicums
    Oil-free roasted red capsicum
        vinaigrette 224
    Stuffed capsicums 152
carrots
    Carrot dip 70
    Carrot-ginger dressing 226
    Carrot walnut salad 78
cauliflower
    Cauliflower soup 97
    Cauliflower with pasta 180
    Roasted cauliflower curry 209
Cavallucci di siena 267
Celery soup 106
cheese
    Cheesy-baked broccoli 208
    substitutes 13, 83
chestnut *see* nuts
Chewy Indonesian rice 175
chia
    egg 31
    Tropical chia breakfast bowl 42
chickpeas *see* beans/legumes
Chilled cucumber soup 98

Chilli and tomato fish 141
chocolate
　Chocolate mousse 243
　Chocolate soft serve 244
　substitutes 11–12
Christmas cake 255
coconut
　substitution 12
cod *see also* fish and shellfish
　Baked crusted cod 139
　Cod steaks in a spicy tomato sauce 126
Coffee cacao banana bread 253
coffee grinder 17
cooking methods 23–5
cottage cheese
　Soy quark 68
courgettes *see* zucchini
Cream of broccoli soup 100
Creamed spinach 211
Creamy avocado pasta with prawns 182
Creamy tofu pasta 181
Creole-inspired salmon 132
crepes and pancakes
　Almond butter and goji berry flapjacks 58
　Blueberry pancakes 39
　Oat-flour crepes 38
Crispy oven fries 205
cucumber
　Chilled cucumber soup 98
curries
　Butternut pumpkin and white fish
　　curry 192–3
　Madras potato curry 195
　Potato quinoa patties with chickpea
　　curry 149–50
　Roasted cauliflower curry 209

D
dairy product substitutes 12–14
Dashi 94
Decadent cocoa cupcakes 269
desserts *see* sweets
dietary restrictions, dealing with other 30
dips
　Baba ghanoush 64
　Bean 66
　Carrot 70
　Roasted eggplant 65

Semi-dried tomato and basil 62
　Soy quark 68
　Spicy sweet potato hummus 67
　Spinach 69
　Vegan tzatziki 219
　Walnut dukkah 63
Dr Swank's diet 5–6, 9, 25
dressings 77, 78, 79
　Balsamic 228
　Carrot-ginger 226
　Flaxseed dijon vinaigrette 225
　Gawler Foundation salad dressing 229
　Ginger miso 222
　Lemon 175
　Mustard vinaigrette 232
　Oil-free roasted red capsicum
　　vinaigrette 224
　Salsa fresca 231
　Silken tofu mayonnaise 220
　Simple honey lemon 227
　Soy yoghurt 223
　tips 223, 229
dried fruit 20
dukkah 63

E
eating out 26–30, 270
　African 27
　Asian 27–8
　at work 27
　fine dining 28
　Italian 28
　Japanese 29
　Mexican 29
　Middle Eastern 29
　other people's houses 30
　vegetarian/vegan 29–30
　what and where to eat out 27
edamame
　Baked wasabi edamame 59
eggplant
　Baba ghanoush 64
　Roasted eggplant dip 65
eggs
　Angel's eggs 72
　Egg white omelette 46–7
　Prawn and pea egg white frittata 144
　substitutes 14, 88, 255

Vietnamese caramelised tofu and egg
    whites 120–1
electric mixer 18
elimination diet 6
Enchilada sauce 216

F

falafels
    Sweet potato falafels 155
fennel
    Roasted fennel with olives and garlic 204
    Sicilian fennel salad 75
Fettuccine Alfredo 183
Fig and pecan biscotti 265
finding recipes 10–11
fine dining 28
fish and shellfish
    Baked crusted cod 139
    Baked salmon in maple mustard sauce 137
    Baked stuffed mackerel 129
    baking 24
    Butternut pumpkin and white fish
        curry 192–3
    Calamari with turmeric and garlic 140
    Chilli and tomato fish 141
    Cod steaks in a spicy tomato sauce 126
    Creamy avocado pasta with prawns 182
    Creole-inspired salmon 132
    Fish lasagne 145
    Fish soup 101
    Fish tacos 146
    Ghanaian fish stew 190
    Gravlax 133
    Herring in oats 128
    Hoisin mackerel 131
    Marinated salmon 136
    Miso mackerel 130
    Moroccan-style fish stew 191
    Pasta puttanesca with tuna 184
    Prawn and pea egg white frittata 144
    Prawn risotto 174
    Saag prawns 142
    Salmon burgers 167
    Salmon flatbread 135
    Salmon in chraimeh sauce 127
    Salmon kedgeree 134
    Salmon parcels 138
    Sardine cakes 124

Seafood chowder 104
    Sizzling trout with crushed potatoes 125
    Smoked salmon, broccoli and lemon
        pasta 186
    sourcing 22, 34
    Thai prawns 143
    Tom yum goong 102
    Tuna and cannellini bean salad 80
    Tuna salad 83
    Tuna with avocado salad 77
    Warm bok choy, prawn and lentil salad 194
flapjacks 58
    Almond butter and goji berry flapjacks 58
flax egg 31
flaxseed 30–1
    Flaxseed dijon vinaigrette 225
flour 9, 19, 24, 235, 237
food processor/blender 17
Fruit crumble 261

G

Gawler Foundation salad dressing 229
gelatine substitutes 14
German-inspired potato salad 88
getting started 17–19
Ghanaian fish stew 190
Ginger miso dressing 222
grains 19
    Whole-wheat grain salad 85
Granola 43
Gravlax 133
Green papaya salad 76
Green salad with pine nuts 89

H

Haricot bean and watercress soup 103
Hassed, Dr Craig ix, 9
herbamare 54
herbs 21
herring see also fish and shellfish
    Herring in oats 128
Hoisin mackerel 131
honey
    Simple honey lemon dressing 227
Honey-mustard glazed green beans 206
household cooking 25
how to use this cookbook 8–9
Hungarian vegetable stew 196

I

ice cream substitutes 13
icing substitutes 14
Indian food
   Indian-spiced chickpeas 151
   Indian-style curried split pea soup 109
Indonesian food
   Chewy Indonesian rice 175
Ingrid's energy bites 55
Ingrid's favourite macro plate 177
intolerances 34
Irish whiskey cake 256
Italian food 28

J

Japanese food 29
Jelinek, Professor George ix–x, 1, 2, 4, 5, 9, 22, 23
juicer 18

K

kale
   Rice with kale 212
   substitute 117
kitchen equipment 17–19
knives 18
Kousmine, Dr Catherine 36
Kousmine-Budwig breakfast 36

L

lasagne
   Fish 145
Layered potatoes 203
Lecsó 196
leek
   Potato and leek soup 105
lemon
   Lemon asparagus 210
   Lemon meringue pie 254
   Lemongrass paste 221
   Simple honey lemon dressing 227
lentils see beans/legumes

M

mackerel see also fish and shellfish
   Baked stuffed mackerel 129
   Hoisin mackerel 131
   Miso mackerel 130
Madras potato curry 195

Marinated salmon 136
McNulty, Jack ix–x, 2, 9, 23
meat substitutes 15
medjool dates 243
menu plan 32
Mexican food 29
   Mexican black bean salad 84
   Mexican stuffed portobello mushrooms 148
   Mexican stuffed squash 157
Middle Eastern food 29
milk substitutes 13
Miso mackerel 130
Miso soup 94
Moroccan food see African food
muffins
   Banana ginger apple 234
   Quinoa blueberry 235
mushrooms
   Broccoli and mushroom quiche with
      wholegrain garlic crust 158–9
   Lentil-mushroom burgers 168
   Mexican stuffed portobello mushrooms 148
   Vegan gravy 218
Mustard vinaigrette 232

N

Naan 236
Neate, Dr Sandra ix
Noémie's pie 160
non-diary
   milk 9
   yoghurt 9
noodles
   Pad Thai 187
   Vietnamese stir-fry 188
Nutrient broth 99
nutritionist advice 33–4
nuts 20
   Almond butter and goji berry flapjacks 58
   Almond cream sauce 156
   Almond shaker 230
   Almond soft serve 244
   Baked fruit and nut clusters 53
   Beetroot and walnut salad 79
   Carrot walnut salad 78
   Chestnut cacao fondant 259
   Chestnut cream 259
   Fig and pecan biscotti 265

Pesto almonds 51
Sweet hazelnut and apple snails 264
Walnut dukkah 63

O

Oat-flour crepes 38
oatmeal
    Overnight oatmeal 44
oil
    flaxseed 30–1
    Olive oil crackers 54
    substitutes 15–16
    use 11, 20
Oil-free roasted red capsicum vinaigrette 224
omelette
    Egg white 46
one-pot meals
    Autumn glory 198
    Butternut pumpkin and white fish
        curry 192–3
    Chickpea stew with silverbeet 197
    Ghanaian fish stew 190
    Hungarian vegetable stew 196
    Lecsó 196
    Madras potato curry 195
    Moroccan-style fish stew 191
    Moroccan-style vegetable stew 199
    Warm bok choy, prawn and lentil salad 194
Onion bhajis 71
oranges
    Bitter orange cacao cake 251
    Orange cake 262
Overcoming Multiple Sclerosis (OMS)
    cooking style, tips and tricks 10–31
    diet 1, 5–7, 8–9, 47
    information 2, 270–1
    nutritional approach 4
    Recovery Program 1, 8
    retreats ix
    snack drawer 57
    website 2, 91
Overcoming Multiple Sclerosis: The evidence-
    based 7 step recovery program 2, 8
Overnight oatmeal 44

P

Pad Thai 187
pancakes see crepes and pancakes

pantry food 19–22
papaya
    Green papaya salad 76
parsnip
    Parsnip mulligatawny soup 107
pasta 19
    alternatives 162
    Autumn glory 198
    Cauliflower with pasta 180
    Creamy avocado pasta with prawns 182
    Creamy tofu pasta 181
    Fettuccine Alfredo 183
    Pasta puttanesca with tuna 184
    Smoked salmon, broccoli and lemon
        pasta 186
    Spaghetti with tofu polpette 185
pastes
    Lemongrass paste 221
peanut substitutes 16
peas see beans/legumes
Peppermint bars 52
Perry, Sandra ix–x, 3, 32, 33–4
Pesto almonds 51
piecrust
    Chickpea 240
pies
    Noémie's pie 160
    Vegan shepherd's pie 118–19
    Zucchini pie 161
Pineapple cake 250
Pita chips 56
Poppy seed strudel 248
potato
    Crispy oven fries 205
    German-inspired potato salad 88
    Layered potatoes 203
    Madras potato curry 195
    Potato and leek soup 105
    Potato enchilada 163–4
    Potato quinoa patties with chickpea
        curry 149–50
pots and pans 18
prawns see also fish and shellfish
    Creamy avocado pasta with prawns 182
    Prawn and pea egg white frittata 144
    Prawn risotto 174
    Saag prawns 142
    Thai prawns 143

prawns *continued*
 Warm bok choy, prawn and lentil salad 194
pregnancy 34
psyllium husk 159
pumpkin/squash
 Autumn glory 198
 Butternut pumpkin and white fish
  curry 192–3
 Butternut pumpkin cake 263
 Mexican stuffed squash 157
 Spiced pumpkin filling 162

Q
quiche
 Broccoli and mushroom quiche with
  wholegrain garlic crust 158–9
quinoa
 Apple quinoa breakfast 37
 Potato quinoa patties with chickpea
  curry 149–50
 Quinoa and pomegranate salad 87
 Quinoa blueberry muffins 235
 Quinoa detox salad 86
 Vegetable protein burgers 171

R
Ramen 95–6
recipe sources 1–2
Rhubarb sorbet 245
rice
 Balkan rice 176
 Chewy Indonesian rice 175
 cooker 18, 199
 Ingrid's favourite macro plate 177
 Prawn risotto 174
 Rice with kale 212
 Warm rice salad 81
rice paper rolls
 Vietnamese summer rolls 73
Roasted eggplant dip 65
roasting 24

S
Saag prawns 142
salads
 Beetroot and walnut 79
 Carrot walnut 78
 Chickpea salad with mint 82

German-inspired potato salad 88
Green papaya 76
Green salad with pine nuts 89
Mexican black bean 84
Quinoa and pomegranate salad 87
Quinoa detox salad 86
Salad in a jar 92
Sicilian fennel 75
Tomato salad with ginger and mint 91
Tuna 83
Tuna and cannellini bean 80
Tuna with avocado 77
Warm bok choy, prawn and lentil 194
Warm rice 81
Whole-wheat grain salad 85
Zucchini and burghul 90
salmon *see also* fish and shellfish
 Baked salmon in maple mustard
  sauce 137
 baking 24
 buying 22
 Creole-inspired salmon 132
 Gravlax 133
 Marinated salmon 136
 Salmon burgers 167
 Salmon flatbread 135
 Salmon in chraimeh sauce 127
 Salmon kedgeree 134
 Salmon parcels 138
 Smoked salmon, broccoli and lemon
  pasta 186
Salsa fresca 231
Salty sesame biscuits 50
sardines *see also* fish and shellfish
 Sardine cakes 124
saturated fat 1, 4, 7, 8, 9, 134, 270–1
sauces
 Almond cream 156
 Barbecue 215
 Caramel 120
 Enchilada 216
 Gooseberry 131
 Sicilian-style tomato 217
 Tahini dill 202
 tips 218, 223
 Vegan béchamel 214
 Vegan gravy 218
 Vegan tzatziki 219

sautéing 23
Savoury popped pumpkin seeds 57
Scrambled tofu 40
seafood *see* fish and shellfish
seeds 20
    Savoury popped pumpkin seeds 57
Semi-dried tomato and basil dip 62
shellfish *see* fish and shellfish
Shepherd's pie, vegan 118–19
Sicilian fennel salad 75
Sicilian-style tomato sauce 217
sides
    Cheesy-baked broccoli 208
    Creamed spinach 211
    Crispy oven fries 205
    Honey-mustard glazed green beans 206
    Layered potatoes 203
    Lemon asparagus 210
    Rice with kale 212
    Roasted cauliflower curry 209
    Roasted fennel with olives and garlic 204
    Steamed brussels sprouts and tahini dill
        sauce 202
    Sugar snap peas with mint 207
Silken tofu mayonnaise 220
Simple honey lemon dressing 227
Sizzling trout with crushed potatoes 125
snacks 26–7
    Almond butter and goji berry flapjacks 58
    Baked fruit and nut clusters 53
    Baked wasabi edamame 59
    Ingrid's energy bites 55
    Olive oil crackers 54
    Peppermint bars 52
    Pesto almonds 51
    Pita chips 56
    Salty sesame biscuits 50
    Savoury popped pumpkin seeds 57
soups
    Cauliflower 97
    Celery 106
    Chilled cucumber 98
    Cream of broccoli 100
    Fish 101
    Haricot bean and watercress 103
    Indian-style curried split pea soup 109
    Miso 94
    Nutrient broth 99

Parsnip mulligatawny 107
    Potato and leek 105
    Ramen 95–6
    Seafood chowder 104
    Sweet potato and avocado 108
    Tom yum goong 102
    Tomato 112
    Vegan split pea and sweet potato 111
sourcing food 22, 33–4
Soy quark 68
soy yoghurt
    Kousmine-Budwig breakfast 36
Soy yoghurt dressing 223
Spaghetti with tofu polpette 185
spices 21
Spicy marinated zucchini 74
Spicy sweet potato hummus 67
spinach
    Creamed spinach 211
    Spinach dip 69
spread and filling substitutes 16
squash *see* pumpkin/squash
Steamed brussels sprouts and tahini dill
    sauce 202
steamer insert 17
steaming 24–5
Stem ginger macaroons 268
stir-fries 23
    Vietnamese stir-fry 188
stock
    Basic vegetable 110
strawberries
    Strawberry mousse 242
    Strawberry mousse cake 249
substitutes
    butter 12
    cheese 13
    chocolate 11–12
    coconut 12
    dairy products 12–14
    eggs 14
    gelatine 14
    ice cream 13
    icing 14
    meat 15
    milk 13
    oil 15–16
    peanuts 16

substitutes *continued*
    spreads and fillings 16
    yoghurt 13–14
Sugar snap peas with mint 207
Sweet and sour haricot beans 153
Sweet hazelnut and apple snails 264
sweet potato
    Spicy sweet potato hummus 67
    Spicy sweet potato pasties 154
    substitute 117
    Sweet potato and avocado soup 108
    Sweet potato and brussels sprout gratin 156
    Sweet potato and tempeh hash 117
    Sweet potato falafels 155
    Vegan split pea and sweet potato soup 111
sweeteners 21
sweets
    Almond soft serve 244
    Apple cinnamon upside-down cake 252
    Baked apples 258
    Banana soft serve 244
    Berry soft serve 244
    Bitter orange cacao cake 251
    Blondie 260
    Butternut pumpkin cake 263
    Cacao bean brownies 257
    Cavallucci di siena 267
    Chestnut cacao fondant 259
    Chickpea shortbread 266
    Chocolate mousse 243
    Chocolate soft serve 244
    Christmas cake 255
    Coffee cacao banana bread 253
    Decadent cocoa cupcakes 269
    Fig and pecan biscotti 265
    Fruit crumble 261
    Irish whiskey cake 256
    Lemon meringue pie 254
    Orange cake 262
    Pineapple cake 250
    Poppy seed strudel 248
    Rhubarb sorbet 245
    Stem ginger macaroons 268
    Strawberry mousse 242
    Strawberry mousse cake 249
    Sweet hazelnut and apple snails 264
    Tiramisu 246–7

T
tacos
    Fish 146
Tarka dal 179
tempeh
    Sweet potato and tempeh hash 117
    Tempeh chilli 116
    Tempeh kebabs with barbecue
      sauce 114
    Vegan shepherd's pie 118–19
Thai food
    Pad Thai 187
    Thai prawns 143
Tiramisu 246–7
tofu 9
    Baked tofu 115
    Creamy tofu pasta 181
    Kousmine-Budwig breakfast 36
    Miso soup 94
    Scrambled tofu 40
    silken tofu 242
    Silken tofu mayonnaise 220
    Spaghetti with tofu polpette 185
    Vietnamese caramelised tofu and egg
      whites 120–1
Tom yum goong 102
tomato
    Sicilian-style tomato sauce 217
    Tomato salad with ginger and mint 91
    Tomato soup 112
toppings
    Almond shaker 230
    tips 223
Triangolini 50
Tropical chia breakfast bowl 42
trout *see also* fish and shellfish
    Sizzling trout with crushed potatoes 125
tuna *see also* fish and shellfish
    Pasta puttanesca with tuna 184
    Tuna and cannellini bean salad 80
    Tuna salad 83
    Tuna with avocado salad 77
tzatziki
    Vegan tzatziki 219

U
unsaturated fat 1

V

vanilla sugar 247
vegan
  binders 12, 159
  recipes, replacing 10–11
  Vegan béchamel sauce 214
  Vegan biscuits 238
  Vegan gravy 218
  Vegan shepherd's pie 118–19
  Vegan split pea and sweet potato soup 111
  Vegan tzatziki 219
vegetables *see also* sides
  Broccoli and mushroom quiche with
    wholegrain garlic crust 158–9
  Hungarian vegetable stew 196
  Indian-spiced chickpeas 151
  Ingrid's favourite macro plate 177
  Lecsó 196
  Mexican stuffed portobello mushrooms 148
  Mexican stuffed squash 157
  Moroccan-style vegetable stew 199
  Noémie's pie 160
  Potato enchilada 163–4
  Potato quinoa patties with chickpea curry
    149–50
  Spiced pumpkin filling 162
  Spicy sweet potato pasties 154
  Stuffed capsicums 152
  Sweet and sour haricot beans 153
  Sweet potato and brussels sprout gratin 156
  Sweet potato falafels 155
  Vegetable protein burgers 171

Zucchini pie 161
vegetarian/vegan restaurants 29–30
Vietnamese food
  Vietnamese caramelised tofu and egg
    whites 120–1
  Vietnamese stir-fry 188
  Vietnamese summer rolls 73
vinaigrette *see* dressings
vinegars 20

W

Walnut dukkah 63
Warm bok choy, prawn and lentil salad 194
Warm rice salad 81
wholefood diet
  definition 33
Whole-wheat grain salad 85
work, things to eat at 27

Y

yeast 9
yoghurt
  soy *see* soy yoghurt
  substitutes 13–14

Z

zucchini
  Spicy marinated zucchini 74
  Zucchini and burghul salad 90
  Zucchini pie 161